NLP for Writers

Bekki Hill

C000171637

Many thanks to all the writers who have challenged, supported and inspired me in my writing endeavours. I would particularly like to thank Sara Grant and Kathy Evans for their enthusiasm and encouragement in their comments on early drafts of parts of this book. My biggest thanks, however, go to my husband and two amazing daughters for their support both in creating NLP for Writers *and in all my writing adventures.*

Bekki Hill discovered NLP when she trained to become a life coach. As a writer, she realized that, just as NLP techniques can be used to gain deeper insight into people's thinking, behaviour and motivation, so they can also be used to gain greater insight into our characters' thinking, behaviour and motivation. Bekki also recognized that aspects of NLP used to build strong communication could be used to consider characters' communication with each other. Furthermore, she identified how an understanding of NLP techniques could strengthen the writer's rapport with their audience – thus engaging them more effectively. Having recognized these possibilities, Bekki gained excellent results exploring the use of NLP techniques in her own work and sharing her ideas with others.

Bekki has published short stories, non-fiction features and wrote a successful coaching column in *Mslexia* for five years. She holds an MA in Writing for Children and has published two other non-fiction books, including *Coach Yourself to Writing Success*, also published by Hodder in the Teach Yourself series.

For further information and inspiration, visit www.thewritecoach.co.uk

Follow Bekki on Twitter® @bekkiwritecoach

Teach Yourself ®

NLP for Writers

Bekki Hill

Also available in ebook

Acknowledgements

Many thanks to the following people who allowed extracts from their work to be used the case studies in this book:

Jon Mayhew – *Mortlock*, Bloomsbury, 2010

V. Kathryn Evans – *Why I hate the wind* post on *My life under paper* blog, January 2012

Thanks also go to Helen Peters for allowing me to quote from our discussions about *The Secret Hen House Theatre* (Nosy Crow, 2012). And to Judy Waite for allowing me to quote her about the role play she used for *The Next Big Thing* (Oxford University Press, 2005) and her work in progress, *Time of My Life*.

Finally, thank you to everyone at Hodder who made this book a reality.

Contents

Introduction: NLP and the writer

NLP is a subject of great breadth and depth which explores human thought, behaviour and communication. It is, therefore, of enormous use to writers, because stories – both fictional and non-fictional – are about human thought, behaviour and communication. Furthermore, writers require strong communication skills to communicate effectively with their audience.

Techniques developed by NLP can be used by writers to:

▶ create more realistic characters

▶ understand their characters' thinking and motivation more completely

▶ develop stronger stories

▶ craft powerful description

▶ engage their audience more effectively

▶ troubleshoot some of their challenges.

At first glance NLP may seem a daunting subject, because it covers such a diverse range of ideas, can be used in many different ways and uses a lot of unfamiliar terminology. This book aims to distil the subject down to show writers how NLP can be used to improve their writing by:

▶ focusing only on what is relevant to writing, i.e. exploring how NLP techniques can be applied to improve areas such as characterization, description, plotting, point of view, exposition and engaging your audience

▶ explaining basic NLP concepts and terminology in everyday language.

NLP can also be very effective in breaking writers' blocks, building motivation and beating procrastination. However,

NLP for Writers will only focus on the craft of writing itself, and will not consider any other uses of NLP, such as by therapists, in business or for personal motivation. If you wish to work on your personal motivation as a writer, see the Further resources section.

What is NLP?

In the 1970s, the mathematician Richard Bandler and the linguist John Grinder drew on a number of disciplines to create NLP as a better way to deliver therapy. NLP was initially used in the 'helping' professions to cure phobias, eliminate bad habits, deal with trauma, relieve stress, build confidence and tackle many other personal challenges. Since then, NLP has spread to be applied to business, personal development, education, health and sport.

NLP continues to evolve, with new techniques and models being added by different people and with different NLP trainers focusing on different techniques and ideas. There is, therefore, no one 'brand' of NLP, but differing branches, each using a majority of the same techniques and principles.

NLP stands for Neuro-linguistic Programming. Unfortunately, unpacking the meaning of this name tends to mystify the subject even further. For those who are interested, a short definition is given in the Guide to terminology. For the purposes of this book, however, it is only important to know that NLP explores human thought, behaviour and communication.

The presuppositions of NLP

A **presupposition** is something we take as a 'given', i.e. something we accept to be true. The presuppositions of NLP embody the founding principles and fundamental beliefs of NLP. However, just as there is no one 'brand' of NLP, there is no one definitive list of presuppositions.

Most NLP trainers and developers list between 10 and 20 presuppositions. This book will only refer to a few core NLP presuppositions that are relevant to the concepts discussed.

These presuppositions will be considered as they become relevant and we will explore one presupposition here, because it runs as a constant thread through this book.

Presupposition: Everyone lives in their own unique model of the world.

The idea that *'Everyone lives in their own unique model of the world'* is one of NLP's core presuppositions and means that we all experience and see the world in our own unique way, unlike the way anyone else does; i.e. no two people see the world as being exactly the same, but perceive and interpret everything in a way that is individual to them.

This presupposition recurs throughout the book because it applies to:

▶ every character

▶ every writer

▶ everyone who watches film or television or reads a book.

It is, therefore, important to bear in mind as you work with this book that you are this book's audience and, as the presupposition identifies, you will have your own unique understanding and interpretation of it. You will therefore find some ideas more interesting or more useful than others and you may agree more or less fully with some of the concepts or conclusions within the case studies.

It is also important to remember that your uniqueness and your audience's uniqueness mean that there is no one 'right' way to write a story. After all, if there was a magic key to penning a best-seller, we'd all write one. If you don't agree with a suggested way of doing something, consider the possibility that the way you are doing something might not be the best way – getting feedback from reliable people might be helpful here too. However, don't make any changes unless you believe the change is right for you, your characters and your story.

Part 1

Characterization and motivation

The driving force behind story

Although real life is random, stories require an internal logic of events linked by a chain of cause and effect. In other words, something happens – usually close to the start – that sets the main character(s) off in a particular – usually new – direction. (This is often referred to as the **inciting incident.**) From then on, the story charts the choices the characters make as a result of the inciting incident and the consequences these choices have. For example, in J. R. R. Tolkien's epic fantasy *The Lord of the Rings*, Bilbo gives Frodo the One Ring. From the moment Frodo receives the Ring, he has to make choices about what he does with the Ring, take action and deal with the consequences of those choices.

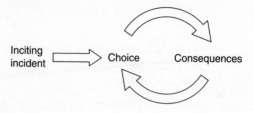

Inciting incident ⟹ Choice → Consequences

Try it now

Read the first chapter of a book you know well or watch the first 20 minutes of a familiar film. Identify what happens in the opening scenes that sets the main storyline in progress. Reflect on the remainder of the story and how the action moves forward in a chain of cause and effect from this point and how the protagonist(s) influences this chain by the choices they make.

It is therefore the choices our characters make that drive our stories forward. The choices our characters make depend on how they perceive and interpret the world.

PERCEIVING AND INTERPRETING THE WORLD

Every time we interact with the world we receive a huge amount of information through our five senses. However, our brains are only able to process a certain amount of this information at any time. We therefore organize our thinking and decide where to focus our attention by subconsciously using the processes of deletion, distortion and generalization (considered in Part 2) and by using **mental filters**.

The mental filters we use are our:

▶ beliefs: what we believe to be true

▶ values: what is important to us

▶ memories: our memories of the past – including past decisions we have made

▶ thinking patterns: the way we think

▶ state: the state we are in. In effect, this means the way we are currently feeling, both physically and emotionally. (See also Chapter 4.)

In other words, **the way we perceive the world will always be filtered by, and therefore influenced by, our beliefs, values, memories, thinking patterns and state.**

Presupposition: Everyone lives in their own unique model of the world.

As discussed in the Introduction, this presupposition tells us that no two people perceive the world as being exactly the same. One reason this happens is because our mental filters are developed by the different life experiences each of us has and the genetic inheritance that makes up our 'personality'. This leads everyone to have a unique filtering system and therefore a unique way of seeing the world and everyone in it.

Consider for a moment how differently a child growing up in a privileged home in Britain and a child growing up in the slums of India are likely to experience the world. Their hugely different experiences will lead to them developing hugely different systems of beliefs, values, memories and thinking patterns. However, even two children of the same sex, growing up in the same family and sharing many of the same experiences, will still experience and perceive the world differently because of their position in the family, their age, the different experiences they do have and because of how their genetically inherited 'personality' interprets what they experience.

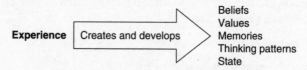

The choices your characters make

Every time a person makes a choice, this too is processed through their personal filtering system of beliefs, values, memories and thinking patterns and influenced by the emotional state they are in. This filtering occurs from small choices we may not even realize we are making, such as how much milk to put on our breakfast cereal, to big decisions, such as changing career or moving house.

Our unique personal system of *beliefs, values, memories* and *thinking patterns* and the *state* we are in filter every decision we face and inform every choice we make. They therefore determine the actions we take.

Because the choices we make are based on our mental filtering system, the actions they give rise to demonstrate to others our:

▶ beliefs: what we believe to be true

▶ values: what is important to us

▶ memories: our memories of the past – including past decisions we have made

▶ thinking patterns: the way we think

▶ state: the current state we are in.

The same is true for our characters:

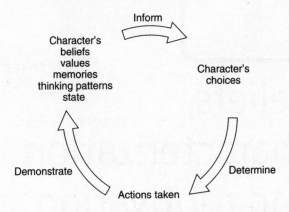

When we create characters whose choices – and therefore the actions they take – are consistently based on their systems of beliefs, values, memories, thinking patterns and their state, our audience will recognize them as real people. If our characters lack any real depth, or make choices that are inconsistent with their beliefs, values, memories, thinking patterns or state, our audience will be unlikely to believe in them or engage sufficiently with them or our story.

In Part 1, the first four chapters will consider four of the components of your characters' metal filtering systems: beliefs, values, thinking patterns and state. The fifth component, memories, is self-explanatory and is also intertwined with the four other filters. Chapter 5, the final chapter in Part 1, will consider making choices. All five chapters will encourage you to explore your characters from different angles, with the overall goal of identifying and understanding your characters' past, how this impacts on who they are, how they think, how they feel and the actions they take.

1

Beliefs, characterization and motivation

In this chapter you will learn about:

▶ *beliefs, and how your characters' beliefs impact on the choices they make and the actions they take*

▶ *ways to explore your characters' beliefs and motivation*

▶ *how your characters' beliefs can support and/or limit the choices they make and the actions they take*

▶ *how your characters' beliefs can impact on your stories.*

Self-assessment: Do you know what influences your characters' belief systems?

Consider the main character or one of the main characters of your work in progress. Give yourself one point for every question to which you answer 'yes'.

Do you know:

1 Who their parents are/were?

2 Where they grew up?

3 What their most important experiences were as they grew up?

4 What their most important adult experiences were?

5 Who their closest friends are, and why they are friends with them?

6 Who their role models are and what they admire about them?

7 What your character is most afraid of?

8 What your character wants most of all?

9 What generalizations they make about themselves? For instance, I'm unlucky, I'm not very confident, I'm ugly etc.

10 What generalizations/philosophies they have about life? For instance, 'You get what you give', 'Nobody can be trusted', 'Life's for having fun', 'God put us on this earth for a purpose', etc.

If you scored 8–10 you have already identified many of the foundations that your character's beliefs are rooted in. If you scored less than 8, you need to spend more time identifying your character's background and working out who they are. Whatever your score, this chapter will help you consider your characters' beliefs more deeply and how these beliefs motivate them throughout your story.

What are beliefs?

A **belief** is something we believe to be true, whether it is true or not. It can be anything from believing giraffes are very tall, that we will write a best-seller, that the Earth is round, to an infinite number of other ideas.

Most of the time we don't think of our beliefs as being something we believe in, but as the truth. Because we believe our beliefs are true, we tend to pay greater attention to experiences and evidence that confirm them, but discount minor experiences that challenge them. However, sometimes we learn about alternative beliefs, or the evidence against our beliefs is so great that we erase or modify them. Looking back in history, we can see that even fundamental beliefs can be proved wrong – people no longer believe the world is flat, that man cannot fly, or that no one can run a sub-four minute mile.

Beliefs and motivation

Although we rarely consciously think about our beliefs, every action we take is based on the beliefs we hold – from martyrs who give their lives for what they believe in, to boiling the kettle before we make a cup of tea because we believe hot water is needed to make one. If you stop for a moment and think about the last thing you did before you started reading this book, you will recognize that you did that thing because of an idea – or several ideas – you believe to be true.

Since every action we take is motivated by the beliefs we hold, the characters in our stories will only appear real to our audience if the actions they take are rooted in their beliefs.

Case study

The futuristic novel *Dark Parties* by Sara Grant tells the story of Neva, who believes her government is manipulating its citizens and hiding the truth about the way the world really is. Neva also believes that her grandmother, who went missing when Neva was a child, is still alive. When Neva's best friend, Sanna, also goes missing, Neva believes she has been taken to a government facility, and Neva and Sanna's boyfriend, Braydon, set off to find her. However, Neva and Braydon have fallen for each other. Out of the blue, Braydon suggests they run away together.

Braydon's proposal offers Neva a course of action that would allow her to leave her past behind and spend her life with the man she loves. However, it would also mean that she would have to abandon her best friend and the search for her grandmother.

Neva wants to say yes to Braydon's proposal more than she has wanted to say yes to anything in her life. However, she still chooses to look for Sanna and not forget her grandmother – demonstrating that she believes that:

* Sanna and her grandmother are still alive
* finding Sanna and her grandmother is more important than escaping the parts of her identity she is unhappy with
* finding Sanna and her grandmother is more important than finding happiness with Braydon.

Try it now

Identify the inciting incident of a favourite book or film. Consider the main character's reaction to this. Identify what belief(s) make them take the course of action they chose to take as a result of the inciting incident.

Key idea

Every action we take is based on the beliefs we hold. However, people rarely identify beliefs as beliefs or recognize that they have them.

Belief systems

We begin to make sense of the world and learn about life in our childhood. As we learn, we build a complex psychological matrix of beliefs that interact with one another. These beliefs agree with and support one another, so it is impossible for us to believe two contradictory ideas at the same time. For example, we can't believe that our ankles are both fat and thin at the same time. Real people's beliefs are therefore always consistent with one another.

If we write a character whose beliefs are inconsistent with one another, our audience will recognize this, either on a conscious or subconscious level. This will erode their ability to believe that character is real. Writers therefore need to have sufficient understanding of their characters' belief systems to make sure that their actions and choices are congruent and believable.

Key idea

When our audience sees a character take an action, it tells them something about what that character believes. If our characters' beliefs are inconsistent with one another or with who that character is, it will erode our audience's acceptance of them.

Our beliefs develop over a lifetime and have their own unique, complex structure and logic. It is therefore insufficient for a writer to simply assign to a character a set of beliefs that agree with one another and that will lead the character to achieve what they want them to achieve within a story. However, because people hold so many beliefs in such complex structures, it would also be impossible for a writer to identify a character's entire belief system. What writers need to do is:

▶ develop a strong understanding of each character's background and who that character is

▶ ensure that each character's beliefs are consistent with one another.

Remember this

As the author of our characters, we do not need to clinically identify a system of beliefs belonging to each of them. What we need to do is have sufficient understanding of each character to ensure that they behave with consistency and in a believable fashion.

Understanding your characters' beliefs

Our childhood is usually the biggest influence on our belief system. Even if we have experiences that significantly change our beliefs when we are older, we are changing them from the viewpoint of the beliefs that have developed in our childhood, rather than placing them on a blank canvas.

Beliefs are mainly generated and modified by the following five influences:

▶ the culture a person grows up in

▶ other people's beliefs

▶ other people's behaviour

▶ significant life experiences

▶ repetitive experiences.

It is important to note, however, that while our culture and other people's influence help create our belief systems, people do not simply take on *all* of the same beliefs as their families, teachers and peers or of the culture they grow up in. Our individual and unique personalities, viewpoints and previous experiences impact on how we incorporate what we learn into our belief system. Different people may have the same experience but form a completely different set of beliefs because of it. For example, if three people see a man walk through a wall, one may believe they have seen a ghost, another may believe it is a trick or optical illusion, and the third that they've drunk too much gin.

By considering the five main influences – named above – that generate and modify a character's belief system, we can create a character portrait that tells us about who our character is and their past experiences. Much of their belief system will remain invisible to us, and even less will be visible to our audience. However, the portrait will help ensure the character reacts and behaves in a believable fashion, congruent with who they are – even if the story grows and changes and they experience situations we had not thought of when we first conceived the story.

CREATING A CHARACTER PORTRAIT
The following two exercises will help you develop characters with realistic belief systems. Use these exercises once you have developed a basic idea of who a character is or the sort of character you want to create.

When you work on these exercises answer all the questions from your character's point of view, making a note of your answers. This will allow you to build a character portrait which you can refer back to and add to as you work on your writing. The questions that can be asked are endless, so as you work through each exercise take time to think of further questions. Writing short stories about any particularly influential life-events can also help you explore a character further.

▶ Upbringing

As our childhood is the place where our belief system is formed, it's important to consider every character's childhood and the impact it has had on their belief system.

Try it now

Answer the following questions for a character you are developing, then consider the impact what you identify has had on them and the experiences it has given them.

❊ Where did they live between their birth and the age of 16?

❊ What was their parents' attitude towards (i) them, (ii) the world, (iii) each other?

❊ What were their relationships like with their siblings and their peers?

❊ Who were their friends? Why were they friends with them?

❊ Who else had a significant influence?

❊ What was their academic experience?

❊ Were they labelled in some way by themselves or others?

❊ What were their worst, best and most influential childhood experiences?

▶ Current situation

If a character is older than 16 (or possibly younger) they may have had adult experiences that have impacted on their childhood belief system. If they have, you might find it useful to draw a timeline of a character's significant adult experiences and consider their impact.

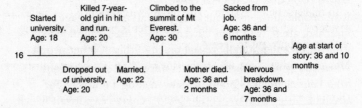

However old your character is, you can consider their current mindset further to help build your understanding of them, and the way they think, by reflecting on their current situation.

Try it now

Answer the following questions and add any insights they give you to your character's character portrait.

* Who are their friends? Why are they friends with them?
* Who supports them? How?
* Who grinds them down/angers/irritates them? How?
* Who do they love?
* Who are their role models? Why?
* What is your character most afraid of?
* What is the worst thing that could happen to your character?
* What's the best thing that could happen to your character?
* What generalizations do they make about themselves, e.g. I'm unlucky. I'm creative etc?
* What generalizations/philosophies do they have about life?

USING KNOWN BELIEFS AS A STARTING POINT

Sometimes characters arrive in our heads with strong opinions before we have a single thought about their life experiences. If you already know a character holds a belief or set of beliefs but are unsure of their past, a good character exploration question to ask can be, 'Why is this belief so important to my character?'

If you are unsure of a character's past, you may also find it helpful to ask, 'What are their most important beliefs?' Consider each belief separately and ask, 'Why is this belief so important to my character?' and 'Where did this belief come from?'.

USING YOUR CHARACTER PORTRAIT

Real people show up in our lives with all their baggage attached, along with their current hopes, dreams and fears. They rarely intentionally reveal much of this to other people. However, others pick up on the tiny clues they subconsciously reveal and gain a fuller understanding of them. The same should be true for your characters; they should turn up on the page with a lifetime of baggage, their worries, dreams and goals. Almost all of this should remain unexplained to your audience, but if the characters are fully present in your mind, they will give away far more to your audience than is specifically explained about them. Thus, they will appear to be real people. If the writer does not know their character well enough, all the audience is likely to see is a two-dimensional cipher.

Other chapters in this book will encourage you to do further work on your character portraits.

Remember this

Characters are like icebergs; only about 10 per cent of what the author knows about them is visible to the audience. But the author knowing the 90 per cent that is out of sight is essential to creating realistic characters that our audience will believe in.

Stories and beliefs

Stories don't just tell us about events that happen – the **action storyline** – they also chart the internal changes characters make as a result of the experiences they encounter in the story. This is called the **emotional storyline**. Because we develop and change our beliefs as we have new experiences, the emotional storyline inevitably charts the characters' beliefs being at least challenged and often changed.

Stories are, therefore, in part an account of changes in beliefs. Changing beliefs can be fundamental to a story. For example, in Dickens' *A Christmas Carol*, Scrooge's beliefs about Christmas are turned on their head. Belief and changes in mindset can also be woven far less obviously into the plot. For example, the narrator of Daphne du Maurier's classic story *Rebecca* – the unnamed second wife of Maxim de Winter – initially believes that her husband is still deeply in love with his first wife – Rebecca – and that he regrets marrying a second time. As events unfold, however, the second Mrs de Winter discovers that Maxim's marriage to Rebecca was nothing but a sham and it is her that he truly loves.

CHANGING YOUR CHARACTERS' BELIEFS

When a character changes a belief, it must be clear to your audience why this has happened. The two events that can change beliefs are:

- ▶ evidence that contradicts what we already believe

- ▶ learning that there are alternatives to what we believe and remodelling our beliefs as a result of this learning.

If a character changes any of their beliefs, the author must provide them with one of these two ways of accomplishing it. Our audience doesn't necessarily have to see the reason a character makes the change prior to the change taking place, but they need to understand why that change happened by the end of the story.

It is important to note here, however, that although characters may be faced with evidence that tells them something is 'true', they may choose to manipulate their belief system to maintain a different belief. For example, a teenage girl may tell herself that the boy she has a crush on, who has told her he doesn't fancy her, really does fancy her but his parents have forbidden him to go out with her.

STRENGTH OF BELIEF

Just like real people, character's beliefs differ in strength – they can be totally convinced of some things while easily persuaded to change their mind about others. If our characters' beliefs change during a story, we need to show opposition to those beliefs that is of an appropriate magnitude. For example, a character living in our reality is likely to take a friend's word at face value if they say they are no longer happily married, but will want proof if that friend says they have seen a UFO.

Key idea

Characters' beliefs often change during the course of a story. When this happens, the author must show how it happens in a logical and believable fashion.

CHARACTERS THAT DON'T CHANGE THEIR BELIEFS

Most stories include at least some characters that make some form of internal change(s) because of their experiences in the story. However, some types of stories need characters who fail to learn from their experiences and therefore fail to change their beliefs or to grow. Instead they remain consistent in upholding the same beliefs and inevitably behave in the same manner.

One important reason for characters to continuously uphold beliefs despite the experiences they undergo is in a series, where it is important that the audience meets the same characters in every new story. Sketch shows and situation comedy characters often need to fail to learn from their experiences because this allows them to continue to behave in ways that deliver the sort of humour their audience expects. Episodic children's stories also need to repeatedly provide a familiar set of characters that the child is expecting to meet whichever book or episode they read or watch, e.g. Paddington Bear and Winnie-the-Pooh.

Your characters' goals and beliefs

As well as informing people what to do when they face choices and need to make decisions, beliefs underpin the goals we strive to achieve. For people to work consciously towards a goal, they need to hold three basic beliefs that support their choice to work towards the outcomes they wish to achieve. They have to believe:

▶ that it is possible to achieve the intended outcome

▶ that they have the ability to achieve the intended outcome

▶ that they deserve to achieve the intended outcome.

Once again, our characters are no exception and these three basic beliefs support any outcome a character strives to achieve. However (just like the beliefs of real people) these three basic beliefs will be founded on a whole raft of beliefs within a character's belief system.

Case study

In the 1994 film *The Shawshank Redemption*, Andy Dufresne is wrongly convicted of the murder of his wife and her lover. Once in prison, Andy works on his goals of escaping - by chipping through his cell wall day after day with a rock hammer - and bringing to justice the corrupt members of the prison staff. The three basic beliefs required can be seen in action here as well as the beliefs that support them.

1 Andy believes it is possible to achieve his intended outcomes
Andy holds a large number of beliefs that support his choice to work towards his intended outcomes. The main ones are:
* even something as small as a rock hammer can cut a tunnel through the thick walls of the prison
* it is possible to keep a growing tunnel secret over a long period of time
* it is possible to steal the necessary documentation to incriminate the prison staff
* it is possible to steal the money the governor has been laundering
* it is possible to escape beyond the reaches of the law that would return him to prison.

2 Andy believes he has the ability to achieve his intended outcomes
Andy could have held many different beliefs about his abilities. Two different sets of beliefs about his abilities could be that:
* he can chip his way out and attempt to live in North America without being rearrested, but be unable to expose the corruption of the prison staff
* he can chip his way out, expose the corruption amongst the prison staff, steal the governor's laundered money and escape beyond the reaches of the law that would return him to prison.

3 Andy believes he deserves to achieve his intended outcomes
Andy believes:
* he deserves his freedom, because he is innocent of the crime he has been locked away for
* he deserves to expose the corrupt prison staff, because they have wronged him and others.

Key idea
For people to work consciously towards a goal, they need to hold three basic beliefs that support their choice to work towards the outcome(s) they wish to achieve:
* that it is possible to achieve the intended outcome
* that they have the ability to achieve the intended outcome
* that they deserve to achieve the intended outcome.

YOUR CHARACTERS' ACHIEVEMENTS

Considering the three essential basic beliefs surrounding what your characters want to achieve can help to:

▶ make your characters and their actions more believable. (If you watch *The Shawshank Redemption*, you will not only find that Andy Dufresne holds even more beliefs relating to his goal of escape than are considered in the case study above, but also see how appropriate the actions he takes are to his character.)

▶ lift constraints you have placed on your character's goals and allow them to achieve more (or at least strive to achieve more) and/or your story to move in different directions. (If you watch *The Shawshank Redemption*, you can see how much greater depth the film has because Andy not only escapes but also works to defy and expose the corrupt prison management.)

▶ reshape or add challenges to a story by considering what would happen if a character didn't believe that they could achieve as much as they currently do.

Exploring beliefs linked to the main goals/outcomes that your characters are striving to achieve can help you to ensure their goals are congruent with who they are and possibly find new avenues and layers to your story.

Try it now

Consider the main character or one of the main characters in your work in progress.

What limits have they put on what they are striving to achieve?
* What is/are the reason(s) they have placed this/these limit(s) on themselves?
* What more could they believe they could achieve in relation to these goals? How could this change your story?
* How could you make their goal(s) stretch them further – mentally, emotionally and/or physically? How could this change your story?
What would happen if your character put a lower limit on what they thought they could achieve? How could this change your story?

What other goals could they aim for?

LACK OF ACTION

Just as a character's beliefs can lead them to set limits on what they think they can achieve, some beliefs can prevent them working towards a dream or goal they desire altogether. Exploring the doubts a character feels and the beliefs that hold them back can help add depth to your work.

SUBCONSCIOUS DESIRES

People may not always be consciously aware or may be in denial about something they want, yet their actions still take them towards achieving it. For example, in the 1990 romantic comedy *Pretty Woman*, millionaire Edward Lewis picks up prostitute Vivian Ward. Vivian leads Edward to see that there is a different way of living than in the cut-throat business world he inhabits and eventually he chooses to change his life. However, it is likely that Edward was already subconsciously seeking a different way of living at the start of the film, otherwise he would not have taken the risk of employing a street prostitute as an escort to take to high-class social events.

The idea of subconscious desires can become a little complex when we consider fictional characters, because the audience learns about a character's desires through their actions. Consequently, it is open to audience interpretation where the line falls between what lies unacknowledged in a character's subconscious and what they are aware of but not admitting to others. However, as the author of a story, you should know what your character thinks on a conscious level – even if some of their subconscious thoughts or memories slip out and surprise both of you when you are working with them.

Remember this

Characters don't have to get what they want, but they have to want what they strive for.

Focus points

The main points to remember from this chapter are:

* Every action we take is based on the beliefs we hold.
* If a character's beliefs are inconsistent with one another or who that character is, this will erode our audience's belief in them. We need to have sufficient understanding of our characters to make sure that they behave with consistency and in a believable manner.
* When a character's beliefs change during the course of a story, the author must show how this happens in a logical and believable fashion.
* For people to work consciously towards a goal, they need to hold three basic beliefs that support their choice to work towards the outcome(s) they wish to achieve: that it is possible to achieve the intended outcome; that they have the ability to achieve the intended outcome; that they deserve to achieve the outcome.
* Beliefs impact both on the goals characters strive to achieve and on the choices and goals they hold back from.

Next step

In Chapter 2, we will consider values, which are another part of our unique, personal system through which we filter our decisions. We will see how values are linked to beliefs and explore how they influence characters' choices, behaviour and motivation.

2

Values, characterization and motivation

In this chapter you will learn about:

▶ *values, and how your characters' values influence the choices they make and the actions they take*

▶ *how values can cause conflict between characters and within a character*

▶ *ways to explore your characters' values*

▶ *how values impact on your characters' goals and their motivation.*

Self-assessment: What are your characters' values?

To identify some of the fundamental principles that a character prizes, consider a scene you have written, or plan to write, where they make an important choice or decision.

1 Ask yourself what they are choosing between.

2 Identify what they gain (or helped others to gain) by making the choice they have. This 'gain' could mean something tangible, such as a money or a new car. It could mean an experience – maybe climbing a mountain or being with the person they love. It could also mean something less tangible, such as gaining respect or knowing they've 'done the right thing'.

3 Check if there's anything else they gain by making this choice, and keep checking until you have identified everything they gain.

4 For the first thing you identified that they gain, ask, 'What's important to them about this?' Unless you have already used a simple descriptor for this (e.g. respect, honesty, support, fun, individuality, security), you should find a further answer to this question.

5 Unless the original or the new answer is a simple descriptor, ask again, 'What's important to them about this?' and keep asking this question of the answers you get, until you have one or more simple descriptors from the first gain you identified.

6 Repeat steps 4 and 5 for each gain you identified in steps 2 and 3.

The simple descriptors you have identified are some of your character's values. They inform the choices your character makes, the actions they take, the goals they pursue and can influence the conflict that arises within your story.

What are values?

Our **values** are the fundamental principles that we believe it important to uphold. They are identified by simple descriptors such as respect, honesty, ambition, adventure, support, peace, creativity, individuality, loyalty. However, while values are basically beliefs, i.e. we believe these principles are fundamentally important although other people may not, our values are far more deeply rooted and therefore far less easily changed than a lot of the other beliefs we hold.

A value is a principle, not something tangible. Things such as money and our family are not values in themselves, but they satisfy values. For example, if we value money, it might be because it brings us security, luxury, recognition, power, freedom or some other value. If you're in doubt about whether something is a value, ask yourself why it's important to your character. If there's a reason underlying why it's important, then the first reason isn't the value. However, there may be more than one value to be found in any one gain or concept. For example, their family may be important to someone because they provide love, security and support.

Presupposition: Everyone lives in their own unique model of the world.

The idea that *'Everyone lives in their own unique model of the world'* tells us that everyone views the world differently. The values we hold and the priority we give them are no exception to this idea. In other words, each person holds their own unique set of values.

VALUES IN DIFFERENT AREAS OF OUR LIVES

When considering values, it's important also to note that we may hold different values in different areas of our lives. For example, the values we believe to be important in our career may differ from those that we believe to be important in relation to our family life. There are values, however, which permeate all areas of our life. These are known as **core values**. The values which we tend to prize only in certain areas of our lives are known simply as values.

Key idea

Everyone has a unique set fundamental principles that are important to them. These principles are known as *values*.

Values and motivation

Our values form the foundations of our beliefs. They are the underlying reason we believe certain things to be true or of importance. They have a strong pull on our emotions and desires and therefore inform the choices we make; and in certain circumstances they can cause us to act without thinking.

Try it now

Consider the main character in a favourite book or film and their reaction to the inciting incident. Ask, 'What is important to them about the choice they make at this point?'

Keep asking the same question of what you find (in the same way that you interrogated the 'gains' in the self-assessment at the start of this chapter) until you have identified the value(s) that underpin the course of action they chose to take at this point.

Key idea

Because values are the fundamental principles that are important to us, they have a strong pull on our desires and emotions and therefore influence our motivation.

Values and conflict

While our values motivate us to take action, sometimes they can cause us to become torn between a choice of different actions to take, because each of the choices upholds one or more of our values.

If we act or consider acting against a strongly held value or values, this will cause internal conflict. Conflict will ensue even if acting against those values satisfies the same value(s) in some other way or satisfies other values that we hold. The stress relating to this conflict can occur while making the choice and/ or after the choice has been made. Equally, if a third party acts against our values, we will experience stress on some level and this may create conflict between us and the third party.

Case study

In the case study in Chapter 1, we considered a scene from the novel *Dark Parties* by Sara Grant. In the novel, Neva, the protagonist, consistently displays the values of *individuality*, *passion* and *loyalty* through the thoughts she has and the actions she takes. If we consider Neva's dilemma again, we can see how these values draw her towards both of the choices she considers.

Neva's dilemma is to choose between:

1 running off with Braydon (the boyfriend of her best friend, Sanna), who she has fallen passionately in love with

2 continuing to search for Sanna, who she believes is held in a government facility.

Neva's original plan also included finding her missing grandmother once she had saved Sanna. Running away with Braydon would stop her doing this too. Furthermore, Neva believes that if she finds Sanna, this will be a step towards exposing the truths the government is hiding and stopping it from suppressing people's individuality.

Choice 1 would:

* satisfy the *passion* Neva feels for Braydon
* satisfy Neva's value of *individuality* by enabling her to have her own identity, rather than being seen as the Minister of Ancient History's daughter.

Choice 2 would:

* satisfy Neva's value of *passion*, because she is passionate about exposing and stopping the government
* satisfy Neva's value of *individuality*, because saving Sanna is a step towards stopping the government from suppressing people's individuality
* maintain her *loyalty* to Sanna and her grandmother.

There is no simple formula relating to values for identifying what choices a real person or a story character will make. In the example above, Neva continues to search for Sanna, and in doing so satisfies more values than running away with Braydon. However, it is not always the option that satisfies the greatest number of values that will win out. The pull that a value has will depend on how highly someone prizes it in relation to their other values, and what other values are involved in the choices available.

Try it now

Consider a scene you have written where a character is torn between two choices.

✳ What values are influencing each side of the character's mental argument?
✳ Which choice wins out?
✳ What are the reasons this choice wins out?

Remember this

Just like real people, our characters rarely identify values as values or even recognize that they have them. They therefore don't explicitly state that they are acting because of a value they hold, but their thoughts and actions give the audience clues about what values – or likely values – they are acting on.

CONFLICT BETWEEN CHARACTERS

Conflict can also arise between people when one person acts against or fails to respect one or more of the other person's values. This isn't necessarily deliberate, but usually occurs because the person showing the lack of respect doesn't uphold that value or values. This, of course, is equally true for our characters.

Key idea

When we act against our values, consider acting against our values or someone else acts against our values, we experience conflict and stress.

Conflict is, of course, the lifeblood of stories. Conflict raises tension, keeping readers turning the pages and film audiences hooked. Both internal conflict (generated by a character's values coming into conflict with one another) and external conflict (generated by two or more characters' values coming into conflict) are therefore fundamental to a story.

Character values and your audience

Although they are unlikely to recognize it on a conscious level, our story's audience forms an understanding of each character's values and the strength of those values from the actions the character takes and the decisions they make.

If a character is happy to act against a value they have previously demonstrated that they hold, this will feel wrong to our audience unless something has happened to give the character a good reason to do it. For example, in the case study above, Neva feels internal conflict when Braydon suggests running away because both the options she considers satisfy some of the same values she holds. However, the reader is likely to be disappointed if she ran away with Braydon because by this stage of the story they have learned of the strength of Neva's value of loyalty. Therefore, although running away with Braydon would satisfy Neva's strongly held values of individuality and passion (which the audience is also aware of), it would act against her value of loyalty. This would contradict the very core of the person the reader has got to know.

NAMING VALUES

As well as having a unique set of values, our uniqueness can lead us to name a value with a particular word, which may mean something entirely different to someone else. Conversely, we may hold a very similar value to someone else but call it by a different name.

When we consider a value, it doesn't matter what name other people would give to that value or what that name means to them. What is important is that we understand what we mean by the names we give our values. The same goes for working with your characters. If you identify them as holding a particular value, it only matters to you what name you give that value. If your audience calls it something different, it doesn't matter – values' names are simply handles to get hold of them by.

Note that this chapter discusses values in terms of a value being described by a single word. However, some values may feel like a combination of several words, or require a description or you may simply associate them with a feeling. However you think about or describe a value is fine; it's just your way of thinking about it. You will never directly tell the audience a character holds a particular value, and your audience will make their own interpretations of your characters' values from the words and actions your characters use.

Exploring your characters' values

Because values are basically beliefs – although far more deeply rooted – they too are held in a complex structure that works in conjunction with the rest of our decision-making processes. It is therefore unlikely that a writer could identify a character's entire value system. However, just as with beliefs, what writers need to do is develop a strong understanding of who each character is. Furthermore, they need to ensure that each of a character's values that they demonstrate to their audience is upheld unless there is good reason for the character to act against the value(s).

Chapter 1 discussed how to build a character portrait to help ensure characters react and behave in a believable fashion congruent with who they are and their growth throughout a story. This portrait will also inform and link strongly to your character's values. Naming and adding a character's values to their character portrait before you write a first draft can help you to:

▶ explore the character further, which will enable you to make them feel more real to your audience (see 'Your characters' values' below)

▶ understand what is going wrong at the revision stage if a character feels at any point as if they are acting 'out of character'.

If you find that a character is acting 'out of character':

▶ name the values and beliefs at play in the scene in question

▶ identify which values and beliefs are given priority by the choice(s) the character makes

▶ ask if the character's choices ring true with their character portrait and in relation to the emotional situation they are in.

If this exploration fails to shed light on your challenge, consider whether the character's actions in the rest of the story are out of kilter with the character's portrait. If so, you may wish to remould the character rather than the story. If you do this, the scene you have been exploring needs to show the character acting in line with the new portrait.

YOUR CHARACTERS' VALUES

This section will help you explore your characters' value systems and explore and define further who they are and how they live their lives. However, be careful not to judge your characters by your own standards. Always allow your characters to be themselves and to value what is important to them. Remember that your characters have their own ideas of what's truly important and that some characters may even hold values that you don't even consider to be values. For example, many people wouldn't value aggression.

Once more, add what you find to the character portraits you created in Chapter 1 in order to have a better understanding of your characters.

Remember this

You only need to create a good understanding of your characters. Don't over-analyse and become obsessed by every single value they might hold or what it is called.

▶ Finding values you already know

You may already recognize that a character holds certain values or you may be at an early stage of development when you're not too sure about your character's past and/or current reality, but have a 'feel' for who they are. If you do get a 'feel' for your characters' values before fully working out their past history, a good character exploration question to ask can be, 'Why is this value so important to my character?'

▶ Finding values from positives

One way to identify a character's values is to consider what they proactively pull into their life and then consider the values that having these things in their life satisfies.

Try it now

Consider your character's life by:

✱ picturing where they live and listing what is important to them in each room of their living space

* 'emptying' their handbag, or 'exploring' their computer files or even their dustbin; list what you find out that is important to their private side
* list the activities they spend their free time on
* list who they spend their free time with.

For each item/person listed, keep asking 'What's important to them about this?' (just as you did in the self-assessment at the start of this chapter) until you get one or more simple descriptors of your character's values.

Remember this

Always allow you characters to be themselves and to value what is important to them.

▶ Finding values from negatives

Another way to identify a character's values is to consider what a character reacts negatively to, as a negative reaction suggests that a value is being dishonoured or confronted.

Try it now

For a character you are working on, consider:
* who they have a bad relationship with. Who upsets them? Who makes them angry?
* what else makes them angry?
* what do they particularly not like?
* what situations make them feel uncomfortable?

Consider which values are being provoked or confronted by the answers you have given.

Remember this

Always allow your characters to be themselves and to value what is important to them.

SHIFTING VALUES

Unless there is good reason for a character to change their values, they must act consistently with them. However, the values they uphold can change, or at least appear to change. This can happen for several reasons.

▶ The character is responding to different situations

Because we hold different values in different areas of our lives, we may prioritize the same values differently in different situations, or not hold a value at all in a certain situation. Holding different values in different areas of our lives is perfectly natural.

▶ The character hides their true values in certain situations

Some people may intentionally display certain values at certain times and not at others. They will always have a reason for doing this and their true values will be:

- ▶ the values they display in private

- ▶ found within their reason(s) for displaying the values they do not truly believe in.

▶ A submerged value is emerging

A story may reveal a character discovering values they already hold, but that had somehow become suppressed. For example in Dickens' *A Christmas Carol*, the ghosts reconnect Scrooge with values he has lost sight of. These values could be described as connection to others, compassion and/or fun. However, you may consider there are other words that describe them better and/or other values at play here too.

POSITIVE INTENTIONS

Presupposition: Underlying every behaviour is a positive intention.

This presupposition may not at first appear to be true. However, when we think about it, we can recognize that everyone acts in accordance with their own agenda – acting primarily because of what they will gain that is important to them. Even those who deliberately cause harm or upset don't do it because they primarily value causing harm or upset, but because they gain something more fundamental – power or confidence, for example. Self-destructive behaviours too will always have, at their root and usually on a subconscious level, a 'good' reason.

Since what is important to us is always underpinned and described by our values, the idea that *'Underlying every behaviour is a positive intention'* is a good reminder that all our characters hold values. Furthermore, even those who behave in the most despicable way may hold values that would make them appear a nobler person if taken out of the context of their actions and other beliefs.

Key idea

As the author of our characters, we do not need to clinically identify a system of values belonging to each of them. What we do need is to have sufficient understanding of each character's values to ensure that they behave with consistency and in a believable fashion.

Priorities, goals and values

Our values are satisfied by what we achieve and when we aim to achieve an outcome, it is because we consciously or subconsciously believe achieving it will in some way satisfy one or more of the values we hold.

Although all our values are important to us, some values will be more important than others. So if we are faced with a choice of different goals to work on, we will choose the one that satisfies the value or values that currently feel most important. However, our value system and real life are usually far more complex than that. For example, more than one value is likely to be connected to any goal we have, or some of the same value(s) may be satisfied by the goals we are deciding between.

Our goals and priorities are likely to be linked to more than one value and possibly more than one area of our life. Furthermore, our fears and habitual thinking patterns may stop us working towards what is most important. The goals our characters pursue, therefore, need to have their foundations in our characters' values, but we need to remain aware of all the relevant factors that might be influencing their decisions. Considering a character's values can help us identify and/or understand the goals and outcomes they aim for and the choices they make. However, creating a list of your characters' values in the order you think these are important to them and blindly following it to inform the choices they make is unlikely to create authentic characters.

Try it now

Think about a book you have read or a film you have watched recently. For the main character (or one of the main characters, if there is no obvious single main character), consider:

* what you think the main character's values are
* what the primary goals are that the main character works towards
* how the main character's primary goals satisfy their values
* how the story explores and tests the main character's values?
* which value(s) the main character has demonstrated they prize most.

Focus points

The main points to remember from this chapter are:

* Everyone has a unique set of fundamental principles that are important to them. These principles are known as values.
* Because values are the fundamental principles that are important to us, they have a strong pull on our desires and emotions and therefore influence our motivation.
* When we act against our values, consider acting against our values or someone else acts against our values, we experience conflict and stress. Conflict raises tension, keeping readers turning the pages and film audiences hooked. Both internal and external conflict generated by conflicting values are therefore fundamental to a story.
* As the author of our characters, we do not need to clinically identify a system of values belonging to each of them. What we do need is have sufficient understanding of each character to ensure that they behave with consistency and in a believable fashion.

✻ Our story's audience forms an understanding of each character's values from the actions they take and the decisions they make. It will feel wrong to our audience if a character is happy to act against any value that they have previously demonstrated they hold, unless something has happened to give them a very good reason to do this.

Next step

In Chapter 3, we will consider frames and meta programs, which are two thinking patterns that NLP identifies as part of our unique mental filtering system. We will see how we use frames and meta programs, along with our beliefs and values, to inform the choices we make and therefore our behaviour and motivation.

3

Thinking patterns, characterization and motivation

In this chapter you will learn about:

▶ *the concepts of frames and meta programs*

▶ *how characters' thinking patterns impact on the way they see the world, their attitudes, the choices they make and the actions they take*

▶ *how thinking patterns can be reflected in dialogue.*

Self-assessment: Do your characters think for themselves?

Consider a scene you have written where at least two characters, but preferably more, need to make a decision.

Mark on a scale of 1–20 how positive each character is about the potential outcome of the situation, where 1 = completely negative, 10 = neutral and 20 = completely positive.

If there are differences between the characters' scores, this shows that they are thinking about the same experience in a different ways. You have therefore, consciously or subconsciously, considered their thinking patterns.

If there is no difference between the scores, you are unlikely to have considered how your characters think, or you are unlikely to have created characters who are sufficiently individual.

Frames and meta programs

NLP considers frames and **meta programs** to be two main filters we use to organize our thinking and decide where to focus our attention. These generally operate outside our conscious awareness, but have a huge impact on our motivation and behaviour.

Key idea

Frames and *meta programs* help us to organize information and decide where to focus our attention. This in turn impacts on our motivation.

Frames: how your characters see the world

If we are to understand something that is happening, we need to understand the context that it is happening in. For example, if we see a man running after another man, our understanding of what is happening depends on the context. If we see them dressed in shorts and trainers on a running track, it means something completely different to us than if we see them in the street and one of them is a policeman.

A frame is basically the context in which we 'frame' an experience. As we grow up, we create frames as we learn about new situations. For example, once we have understood what an athletics race consists of, we create a frame that tells us what we expect to experience when we next see an athletics race and this means we don't need to spend time working out what is happening.

Frames, however, don't just help us to recognize what is happening. They tell us how to respond. And because they tell us how to respond, they influence our motivation. For example, if you saw a man in a restaurant kitchen with a knife, you would probably stay calm and carry on with what you were doing. If you saw a man in the street with a knife, you would probably become anxious and take some form of action motivated by your anxiety.

Remember this

Frames don't just help us recognize what is happening. They tell us what attitude we need to take and what response to give in that situation.

As we become older our responses become reinforced by repeated experiences. Consequently, we make assumptions more quickly about situations we perceive to be familiar and also habitually frame life in certain ways. For example, one person may habitually use what NLP refers to as an 'outcome' frame when they find themselves in a situation where things are going wrong, i.e. their attitude is to look for solutions to make things better when things go wrong. Another person may habitually use what NLP refers to as a 'blame' frame when they find themselves in a situation where things are going wrong, i.e. their attitude is to look for someone to blame for what is going wrong.

$$\text{Frame} \xrightarrow{\text{Influences}} \text{Attitude} \xrightarrow{\text{Influences}} \text{Action(s) taken}$$

When writers create characters, they can use the idea of frames to give characters' dominant attitudes to life in general and in the way they frame certain situations. As mentioned already, as well as giving context, frames inform us how to respond. This is because we don't just frame a situation, but also consider how we fit within that frame. Each situation we frame therefore also reflects back to us how we see ourselves in that situation. Therefore when we habitually see the world in a certain way, we also habitually see ourselves in a certain way.

Case study

If we consider four of the main characters in A. A. Milne's *Winnie-the-Pooh* stories, we can see how the way they habitually frame the world informs their attitudes and, in turn, how this influences the actions they take.

Character	Pooh	Piglet	Eeyore	Tigger
Tends to frame the world as	Confusing	Scary	Bad/out to get him	Exciting
General attitude to life	Expects to get things wrong	Fearful	Negative	Embraces life
General attitude to self	Not very clever	Weak	Unlucky	Fabulous
When faces a challenge, tends to	Dither/look to others	Hide	Do nothing	Jump in head first

Note that this case study considers the characters' **habitual** frames and their usual reactions. Each different situation will cast influence. Some situations will lead characters to move away from a habitual thinking pattern and apply different frames. For example, Pooh will not frame the existence of a jar of honey as 'confusing'. Pooh is more likely to frame a jar of honey as highly desirable, or something similar. His strong sense of desire is likely to override his general self-doubt and he will take a highly proactive attitude to acquiring it.

Try it now

Take four main characters from your work in progress. At the start of your story:
* how do they generally tend to frame the world?
* what is their attitude to life?
* what is their attitude towards themselves?
* how do they usually behave when they face a challenge?
You may find some of these questions easier to answer for some characters than others.

Presupposition: Everyone lives in their own unique model of the world

When we consider the frames different people use, we can see how different people can experience the same thing and yet perceive it in completely different ways. This reinforces the presupposition that we all live in our own unique model of the world.

Key idea

Defining how a character frames life in general and particular situations will help inform us about how they are likely to behave in general and in specific circumstances.

DEVELOPING CHARACTERS

Considering the dominant or habitual frames a character uses and the way they frame certain situations can be useful for character development. We can:

▶ create a character who uses particular frames, then get to know them better by considering how their past could have led to this

▶ consider significant or repeated past experiences in a character's profile (see Chapters 1 and 2) and identify what frames they are likely to have created

▶ observe and identify which frames we have unconsciously placed in our characters' thinking patterns.

If you recognize that a character uses particular frames or devise a character who uses particular frames, you can identify how they would think in a given situation and therefore the actions they would be likely to take.

Try it now

Take a character from your current work in progress. Consider what they would think and do, by imagining a scene where they:
* are asked to skydive
* go to a party
* are asked for money by a beggar.

What does their response to each situation tell you about the frames and/or attitudes they apply to skydiving, dangerous situations, parties, socializing, and homeless people?

If you have created a character profile (see Chapters 1 and 2) for this character, see if you can identify which beliefs, values and/or past experiences have led them to create the frames/attitudes you have identified.

Remember this

Frames are basically beliefs that inform us about how to respond to a situation. Just as with any beliefs, our characters need to consistently uphold the frames they have developed, unless something happens to make them reframe the situation.

REFRAMING

Reframing means changing the way you perceive an event so that you change what it means to you and how you see yourself within the situation. For example if you habitually see not achieving something you set out to achieve as failure, you could reframe it as a learning experience. This new perception is likely to change your attitude and the resulting actions you take.

Frame	Likely attitudes	Likely to see self as	Likely actions
Failure	I failed I can't do it Negativity Reduction in perception of self-worth/confidence/esteem	A failure	Give up Carry on, but with a more negative attitude
Learning experience	It didn't work out this time What have I learned? What can I do differently to achieve this?	A learner On a journey	Identify what didn't work and why Look for new solutions Try again

NLP has developed reframing techniques which help people to change the way they see situations that they are currently interpreting in a way that is unhelpful to them. However, reframing wasn't invented by NLP; there are times when we all naturally reframe events or the meaning we've assigned to something. An example would be realizing with hindsight that we had overreacted to a situation which wasn't as important as we thought it was at the time. Jokes also often use reframing, starting off using one particular frame and then adding some kind of twist that reframes the context and therefore the meaning.

CHARACTERS AND REFRAMING

In the Chapter 1 section 'Stories and beliefs', we considered how stories often chart their characters' changing beliefs. This applies equally to the frames characters use, as frames are basically beliefs about how to think about and respond to a situation. Changing their beliefs can, and often does, lead characters to reframe meanings or situations. If you consider again the examples given in 'Stories and beliefs' in Chapter 1, you will see that:

▶ Ebenezer Scrooge reframes Christmas; this leads to a change in his attitude and actions

▶ the narrator in *Rebecca* reframes her relationship with her husband and her marriage when she learns the truth about Rebecca; this leads to a change in her attitude to her husband and her marriage and her expectations of them.

Character	Original frame	Attitude	Sees self as	New frame	Attitude	Sees self as
Scrooge	Christmas is a waste of time and money	Ba, humbug!	Isolated	Christmas is to be celebrated and enjoyed	Let's celebrate!	Connected
Narrator in *Rebecca*	My husband is still in love with Rebecca	Sad	Unwanted	My husband loves me	Happy	Loved

Try it now

Return to the four characters you considered in the first Try it now exercise in this chapter, which explored the ways they framed the world at the start of your story. Now consider the end of your story.

✶ How do they tend to frame the world?
✶ What is their attitude to life?

* What is their attitude towards themselves?
* How are they likely to behave in the future when they face a challenge?
* Have any of your characters reframed the way they see the world?
Also consider their attitudes and the frames they place on less general situations throughout the story. Is there anything (else) they have reframed?

Key idea
Reframing means changing the way you perceive an event so that you change what it means to you.

Meta programs: how your characters think

NLP's concept of meta programs describes how we organize our thinking. Meta programs also help us decide where to focus our attention. Most meta programs come in pairs of bipolar opposites. However, most people don't operate at the extremes, but somewhere along a spectrum between the pair of opposites.

Over 50 meta programs have been defined, and there are probably many more, but we will consider only a handful here. When you first read through the examples below, don't get bogged down in the detail. Once you have read enough to understand the concept of meta programs, read the rest of the chapter and return to the detail when you are considering your characters.

▶ Best-Case vs Worse-Case Scenario

If we are using the Best-Case Scenario thinking style, we first consider the positives, possibilities and opportunities within a situation. If we are using the Worst-Case Scenario style, we focus on the problems, dangers, threats, difficulties and challenges of a situation.

People using the Best-Case Scenario thinking style are therefore more likely to find something positive within any given situation. They are also more likely to take part in new and/or potentially dangerous experiences than those using the Worst-Case Scenario style.

▶ Towards vs Away From

People using the Towards thinking style focus on what they want or want to achieve, and direct their time and attention to accomplishing it. The Away From thinking style focuses on what people don't want and want to get away from.

People who habitually use the Towards thinking style will be most strongly motivated when they have a goal to aim for. However, sometimes people can be so Towards-focused that they don't pay enough attention to the possible pitfalls or dangers of a situation. They can also become easily demotivated if they don't have a target to aim for and will respond better to a task if told that they need to achieve something rather than that they have a problem to solve.

Away From thinking leads people to direct their time and attention to getting away from or rid of what they don't want. People who habitually think in this way will therefore be most strongly motivated when there is something they need to escape or avoid, or a problem to solve. They are often good at spotting the pitfalls and dangers of a situation, but if they become too focused on resolving issues or avoiding potential problems, they can fail to prioritize. They have a tendency to be cautious.

▶ Big Chunk vs Small Chunk

This thinking is used to filter details and is sometimes called the **General–Specific** filter. It concerns the level of generality or specificity in the way we think.

Big Chunk thinking considers the bigger picture. People who habitually think Big Chunk tend to process things all in one go and may have difficulty following a step by step sequence. They are motivated by whole ideas or experiences, bored by the nitty-gritty and may switch off if bombarded by too much detail. They can miss out or fail to consider important details.

Small Chunk thinking focuses on details. People who habitually think Small Chunk look at detail in an idea or situation. They are motivated by taking things step by step and often get wound up in the details. They may find it hard to think holistically or to understand something in its entirety.

Remember this

▶ Internal vs External

This meta program is about how we reference our own perceptions. If we are thinking with the Internal filter, we check in with ourselves to decide how we feel about something rather than looking for others' opinions. If we are using the External filter, we check in with others' reactions, opinions or other external evidence to form our opinions.

People who habitually use the Internal filter are likely to be self-starters and are motivated by their own wishes. They will seek out information from external sources and then come to their own conclusions. This sort of behaviour can lead to rejection of information and ideas that don't fit with what they already believe. They don't like being told what to do and, at the extreme, people with a dominant Internal thinking filter don't care what other people think. Using the Internal filter is related both to self-confidence, when it is being used in a healthy way, and sociopathy when it is not.

People who habitually use the External filter will seek out others' advice and support. They are more likely to be motivated by other people's ideas or encouragement and can feel lost or lack direction without it. Use of External thinking is related both to compassion, when it is being used in a healthy way, and low self-confidence and co-dependency when it is not.

▶ Self vs Other

This filter considers how much people instinctively notice and respond to other people. People running the Self filter don't appear to be aware of the reactions and behaviours of those around them. They tend to talk about themselves and place importance on what they have to say, failing to show interest in other people.

When someone is using the Other filter, they respond well to other people's reactions and non-verbal signals. They tend to find it easy to relate to other people, to take their views into consideration and to be thoughtful and understanding.

▶ Options vs Procedures

People who operate using the Options filter literally like to have a lot of options open to them. People who operate using the Procedures filter are motivated by having a specific focus.

People operating the Options filter are motivated by variety, new ideas and bending the rules. Freedom tends to be important to them, they like to be in control of their own future and they are good at starting things, although not at finishing them. However, they can shy away from making decisions as this cuts down the options available to them.

People operating the Procedures filter are likely to take things step by step, follow instructions and finish what they've started. They like to follow rules and can feel overwhelmed when there is too much choice.

▶ Proactive vs Reactive

If someone is operating a Proactive thinking style, they jump right in when a challenge arises or they recognize something needs to be done. Reactive thinking leads people to stop and analyse a situation when a challenge arises and to wait for others to initiate action.

When people operate with a Proactive filter, they don't wait for others and can be good at going out and getting a job done. However, at the extreme, they can bulldoze people into doing things their way.

If someone is operating Reactive thinking, they will assess and analyse a situation before they act. They often wait for others to take the first step and at an extreme they can over-analyse and fail to take action at all.

Remember this

Operating any particular thinking style is not intrinsically good or bad. However, the styles being used can have positive or negative consequences for a person and those around them.

Your characters' thinking styles

Meta programs can be context-specific, i.e. the thinking styles we use vary depending on the situation we are in. However, we also tend to have dominant thinking styles. Writers can therefore give characters habitual thinking styles and use these as character 'traits' that impact on their characters' motivation and other aspects of their character.

Case study

In the 1984 film *Aliens*, Ellen Ripley, the only survivor of a previous alien encounter, and a team of marines, including a private called Hudson, search for survivors of a space colony attacked by aliens. They find only one survivor – a young girl – and are attacked themselves, winding up trapped in the colony complex.

When the group learns that they have 17 days to wait before a rescue mission is sent, Private Hudson panics and says they don't stand a chance. However, Ripley points out that the girl they've found survived longer with no military training, and Ripley devises a plan to seal off the complex.

Shortly afterwards they discover that the processing station was damaged as they battled the aliens and will soon detonate with the force of a thermonuclear weapon. Hudson panics again. But Ripley calmly devises a plan, along with a robot, Bishop, to retrieve a drop ship from their mother ship so they can escape.

Ripley's coolheaded planning demonstrates her use of the following thinking styles:

Best-Case Scenario thinking
* If the girl survived, they can.
* They can secure the complex and keep themselves safe while they wait to be rescued.
* They can escape the explosion.
* They can acquire the drop ship.

Towards thinking
* In the face of the first challenge, Ripley considers how they can stay safe.
* In the face of the second challenge, Ripley considers how they can escape.

Private Hudson's panic and fear demonstrate his use of the following thinking styles:

Worst-Case Scenario thinking
* The aliens will get in and defeat them.
* The explosion will kill them.

Away From thinking
* In the face of the first challenge, Hudson only thinks that they need to get away from the aliens.
* In the face of the second challenge, Hudson's Away From thinking doesn't even kick in as he assumes they will die.

Note:
* The Best-Case Scenario style is not necessarily the best way to think. In certain circumstances, Worst-Case Scenario thinking is more useful, e.g. when gathering equipment to climb a mountain.
* The Best-Case Scenario and Towards styles often work as a pair and the Worst-Case Scenario and Away From styles often work together. But this is not always the case.
* Ripley is also using a *solution-focused frame* while Hudson uses a *problem-focused frame*.

THE META PROGRAMS YOUR CHARACTERS USE

Identifying the thinking styles your characters habitually use can help you identify how they would think in a given situation and the actions they would be likely to take.

Recognizing a character's habitual thinking styles can also help ensure that they act 'true to character' throughout your story.

Try it now

Identify one of the characters from your work in progress who habitually uses one or more of the thinking styles described earlier. What would they think and what would they do:
* if they were trapped on the 50th floor of a burning skyscraper?
* if they found out their husband/wife/partner/best friend had got them into colossal debt?

* if they had to give a speech in front of one of their lifelong heroes?
* if they had to organize a wedding?

Remember, not all thinking filters are used in all situations. So don't worry if you can't describe a reaction to all of the above.

Key idea

Identifying the thinking styles a character uses in life in general or a particular situation can help us identify how they would react in other situations.

Experimenting with extremes of different meta programs may also be helpful when you are trying to get to grips with a character you are building. As you do this, it may even trigger ideas for how this character's thinking style(s) might impact on or even improve the plot.

EMPLOYMENT, THINKING STYLES AND SELF-PERCEPTION

Our employment, or lack of it, usually has a big impact on our life, our self-perception, our beliefs about how capable we are and our self-worth. The same, of course, is true for our characters. Giving your character a job that is either well-suited or ill-suited to a thinking style they predominantly use will allow you to influence their self-perceptions. Even if a character is a child, their capabilities at school and/or within their peer group shape their view of who and how important they are.

Considering the thinking styles a character uses can also be a great way to help identify a career/job that is congruent with a character's self-perception.

Try it now

List the sort of jobs a Small Chunk thinker would be suited to. What jobs might they not be suited to?

THE LANGUAGE OF META PROGRAMS

When people are using particular thinking styles, they have a tendency to use certain language or speak in a particular way. The more extreme their use of the filter, the more obvious this is likely to be.

Filter running	Language
Towards	Places emphasis on what can be accomplished rather than what could go wrong. Uses words such as 'get', 'gain', 'achieve', 'obtain'.
Away	Tends to describe the challenges they face as obstacles, issues or problems. Uses words like 'avoid', 'overcome', 'solve', 'prevent'.
Big Chunk	Talks in broad strokes about whole concepts and abstract ideas. Their explanations lack detail.
Small Chunk	Includes a lot of detail. Uses words like 'precisely' or 'exactly'.
Internal	Likely to tell you what they think and to make what they are saying sound as if it is fact rather than opinion.
External	Uses language that seeks out others' opinions. Uses phrases such as 'What do you think?' and 'Do you agree?'
Options	Tends to come up with a lot of ideas and suggestions that have not been well thought out.
Procedures	Tends to like to explain things one stage at a time and in a logical order.
Proactive	Has a direct style of speech. Uses short sentences and talks as if they are in control of their world. Uses phrases like 'Go for it', 'Let's do it', 'What are we waiting for?'
Reactive	Uses longer sentences, likes to analyse and uses words such as 'clarify' and 'consider'. Speaks as if the world is in control of them.

Remember this

The frames and thinking styles we choose to use are influenced by our beliefs, values, memories and the state we are in.

Focus points

The main points to remember from this chapter are:

* Frames and meta programs help us to organize information and decide where to focus our attention.
* Frames and meta programs generally operate outside our conscious awareness, but have a huge impact on our motivation and behaviour.
* Defining how a character frames life in general and in particular situations will help inform us about how they behave in general and in specific circumstances.
* Reframing means changing the way you perceive an event so that you change what it means to you.
* Identifying the thinking styles a character uses in life in general or in a particular situation can help us identify how they would react in other situations.

Next step

In Chapter 4, we will explore the NLP idea of 'state' and how this impacts on our characters' choices, behaviours and motivation. We will also consider how a character's state can be manipulated in order for them to make choices and decisions that their beliefs, values and habitual thinking patterns would not normally lead them to make.

4

State, characterization and motivation

In this chapter you will learn about:

▶ *the concept of state, and how a character's state influences the choices they make and the actions they take*

▶ *how you can influence your characters' state to manipulate the choices they make and the actions they take*

▶ *the concept of anchors, and how they impact on your characters' state.*

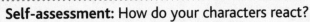

Self-assessment: How do your characters react?

Read through a scene in your work in progress where one of your main characters has one or more of their values confronted or fulfilled.

1 How does the character feel when this happens?

2 Name any emotional reaction(s) the character has.

3 How do you show these reactions to your audience?

4 How does the character's behaviour change when their value(s) is/are confronted or fulfilled?

If you are instinctively working with your character's 'state', then:

1 Your character will have had an emotional reaction when their value(s) were confronted or fulfilled.

2 These emotion(s) should have been conveyed to your audience – although that doesn't mean you have to name the emotion(s).

3 Your character's behaviour should also have been influenced in some way.

If these things have not happened, then you aren't working on a deep enough level with this character.

What do we mean by 'state'?

When NLP talks about 'the state we are in', it refers to the sum total of our reaction to everything we perceive and the way we are processing it at any given moment. This means our reaction not only to the myriad external influences we are consciously aware of, but also to an even greater number of influences we are subconsciously aware of, plus all our internal neurological and physical responses and processes.

State = The external influences we are consciously aware of + The external influences we are subconsciously aware of + Our internal neurological responses and processes + Our physical responses and processes

This might feel like a huge concept to get hold of, but 'the state we are in' is simply our final reaction to all of these influences. Therefore 'the state we are in' effectively means how we are currently feeling.

Key idea

When NLP talks about the *state* we are in, it refers to the sum total reaction to everything we perceive and the way we are processing it at any given moment. This can be interpreted in more simplistic terms as how we are currently feeling.

While most states can be expressed as the way we feel, we usually only acknowledge that we are in a particular state when our feelings are of a certain intensity. However, if we stop to check the state we are in throughout the day, we will recognize that we are always in one state or another.

Try it now

What state are you in right now?

Maybe you are:

* inquisitive about what you're going to learn in this chapter
* questioning if you're going to learn anything, because the self-assessment said you are working well with character 'state'
* relaxed
* in some other state related to reading this book
* in a state related to something that has nothing to do with this book.

When you name a state, it doesn't have to be the name of a single emotion or feeling. For example, you could be nauseous, nervous and on high alert.

Remember this

We are always feeling something, even though we often don't consciously acknowledge it.

CHANGING STATES

In a typical day, people go through many changes of state. Some states may only last for a few minutes or seconds, while others may last for hours. Some will be positive and enjoyable, others will be negative and some will be quite neutral. For example, we may wake up looking forward to the day, but get angry because our two-year-old throws their breakfast all over the floor and makes us late leaving for work. Our mood may lighten as we hit all the green lights and catch up on the time we lost. We may be relaxed by the music playing on the car radio and excited when we drive into the car park and see the colleague we are having an affair with ...

Try it now

Reflect on the past 24 hours and the experiences you have had. Name some of the different states you have been in. If you find it difficult to remember, check in with yourself a few times over the next 24 hours to see what state you are in.

Remember this

Our state changes throughout the day.

Character, state and behaviour

The state we're in not only affects how we feel, but also how we behave. For example, when we're unsure, we may become cautious; when we're panicked, we may act quickly.

Presupposition: Everyone lives in their own unique model of the world.

Our unique understanding of the world can lead different people to enter different states as a reaction to the same experience. It also means that different people can react differently to being in a similar state. For example, some people may shout when they are angry, others may cry, others may sulk.

Since state is governed by our unique personal make-up, writers need to ensure that the states which arise within a character are appropriate for that character given the circumstances they are in. The behaviour of each character must also be appropriate for that character in the state they are in. This highlights once more how developing sufficient understanding of your characters and their past experiences is key.

The state we are in itself also colours the way we currently see the world and therefore influences the state we move to as the result of an experience. For example, if someone is already upset, they may become more upset by something that wouldn't matter to them on a day when they were feeling chilled.

Writers therefore need to ensure characters react appropriately in relation to:

▶ who they are

▶ the state they are in.

Key idea

The state a character is in depends on who they are and on their current situation. The state they are in will influence how they behave.

If you are well in tune with a character, you will automatically know how that character feels as they encounter different experiences. You will also allow your characters to react appropriately to the state they are in. However, beginner writers can make two major mistakes when it comes to writing about their characters' states.

▶ Mistake 1: Creating characters who only feel and act as the writer would

There's nothing to say a character can't feel or react the way you do. However, if you're going to write a character that does this, it's important to be aware of what you're doing and to have good reason for doing it. Don't create a character in your image because it's less hassle to write a character that way.

▶ Mistake 2: Making characters feel and act as the plot requires

Sometimes writers are so focused on their plot that they make their characters react in the way they need them to for the story to progress. This can result in characters that do one or more of the following:

▶ act out of character

▶ react inappropriately for the way they feel

▶ behave inappropriately for the prevailing circumstances

▶ fail to react when they should be reacting, because their reaction would be inconvenient to plot progression.

Try it now

Read through a chapter of your work in progress. Note how the main character's state changes through the chapter.

✳ What influences each change of state?

✳ Are these changes of state appropriate to the influences on the character?

✳ How does the character react to their changes of state?

✳ Are these reactions appropriate to the state change that has occurred?

Developing character profiles (see Chapters 1–3) should help you tune in to your characters. This will help you to recognize instinctively how they would feel, think and behave. Character profiles can also be used to help check that characters are reacting appropriately.

Key idea

Whatever circumstances a character encounters, their feelings, reactions and behaviour must always be appropriate for who they are and what they are experiencing.

CONVEYING WHAT YOUR CHARACTERS FEEL

Writers are sometimes so wrapped up in the feelings of their characters that they forget to convey their characters' feelings to their audience. Always ensure you give sufficient information for your audience to understand what you want them to know about a character's state. A character's state can be revealed by:

▶ the thoughts they share

▶ what they say

▶ the choices they make

▶ the actions they take

▶ non-verbal signals.

Various chapters in this book explore these ideas further.

Remember this

You may understand the emotions a character feels, but it is important to ensure your audience understands them too.

Manipulating characters

Although characters need to behave 'in character', this does not mean they can only behave in certain ways. If you need a character to take an action that they would not normally take, you can put them in a situation that creates a state in which they would take that action. However, you must ensure that:

▶ the plot doesn't take some unlikely turn just to fit in this occurrence

▶ your audience understands the changes in your character's state and the reasons they choose to take the action(s) they take – although this understanding does not necessarily have to be recognized on a conscious level.

Case study

If you review the case studies of the scene from Sara Grant's novel *Dark Parties* that we explored in Chapters 1 and 2, you will note that although Neva holds a strong value of loyalty, she allows a romantic relationship to spark between herself and her best friend's boyfriend, Braydon. This relationship is clearly dishonouring her loyalty to her best friend. However, Grant justifies Neva's behaviour and makes it believable by manipulating Neva into accidentally kissing Braydon, and experiencing their first kiss with such passion that every time she sees him, this passion is rekindled.

Manipulation 1: Anyone who prizes loyalty as highly as Neva wouldn't normally kiss their best friend's boyfriend. However, the kiss between Braydon and Neva happens at the 'dark party' where Neva cannot see who is kissing her.

Manipulation 2: When she experiences the kiss, Neva is in a heightened state of excitement and anxiety, because:

* the purpose of the dark party is to find people who will help Neva and Sanna act illegally; in staging it, they are crossing the threshold from simply talking about taking action against the government to actually taking action
* although it is dark, the presence of other people creates a sense that Neva may get caught
* the kiss is illicit; Neva is kissing a man who isn't her boyfriend and enjoying it. (Grant justifies Neva's disloyalty to her boyfriend because the relationship is over and now exists in name only.).

Manipulation 3: The entire interaction between Neva and Braydon is sexy and passionate.

Grant therefore effectively manoeuvres both her audience and her character into believing that Neva can't help but have feelings for Braydon despite her fierce loyalty to her best friend.

Key idea

A writer can manipulate circumstances to get the reactions they want from their characters.

Try it now

Create a scene for a character you know well where they act against type by doing one of the following.
* If they would never steal, make them steal something.
* If they are prone to stealing, put them in a situation where they don't steal something that they usually would.
* If they fall between the two types above, get them to steal something really expensive that normally they would never dream of taking.

If you're unable to identify a suitable incident, brainstorm possible scenarios that might push the character to act 'out of character'.

Write the scene, ensuring you show the state change(s) in your character.

Using anchors to create immediate state changes

An **anchor** is a stimulus that instantly triggers a particular action or state. Some anchors may be specific to a particular person, while others are more generally influential.

Anchors can be something we see, hear, touch, taste or smell. For example:

Sense stimulated	Anchor and reaction
Seeing	Spiders make many people feel fear
Hearing	Music can evoke emotional reactions
Touching/Feeling	Sitting in a comfortable chair makes most people feel more relaxed
Tasting	The taste of freshly baked bread gives many people a homely feeling
Smelling	The smell of hospitals often makes people feel negative in some way

Key idea

An *anchor* is a stimulus that triggers a particular action or state in a person, without them even thinking about it.

Anchors are not something writers need to pay particular attention to. However, it is worth being aware of them because they can instantly influence our emotional state and our actions. They can therefore be used to instantly change a character's state and/or influence the actions they take.

Try it now

Consider your work in progress.
* Name each key character's worst fear.
* What anchor(s) would/could trigger each of these fears?
* What does each character feel when they see the anchor that triggers their fear?
* What does each character do when they see the anchor that triggers their fear?

Focus points

The main points to remember from this chapter are:

* When NLP talks about 'the state we are in', it refers to the sum total reaction to everything we perceive and the way we are processing it at any given moment. This can be interpreted in more simplistic terms as how we are currently feeling.

* The state we are in impacts on how we behave.

* Whatever circumstances a character encounters, their feelings, reactions and behaviour must always be appropriate for who they are.

* A writer can manipulate circumstances to get the reactions they want from their characters.

* An anchor is a stimulus that triggers a particular action or state in a person, without them even thinking about it. Anchors can be used to instantly influence a character's state and/or the actions they take.

Next step

We have now explored the four filters that influence the choices our characters make. Chapter 5 will explore the process of making choices and how characters can be developed and explored through the choices they make.

5

Actions speak louder than words

In this chapter you will learn about:

▶ *the concept of strategies, and how strategies impact on the choices your characters make and the actions they take*

▶ *how both characters' routines and the new strategies they develop demonstrate who they are, how they think and where they've come from.*

Self-assessment: Are your characters sufficiently different and individual?

Consider one of your main characters and answer as many of the following questions as you can for them.

1 What is their morning routine from waking up to leaving the house/getting on with their work inside the house? Briefly identify the order in which they do these things.

2 What are their religious routines?

3 How do they get to work?

4 What events do they celebrate every year?

5 What do they do to relax/have fun?

6 When and where do they eat lunch?

7 What do they collect or save?

8 Who do they visit regularly?

9 What superstitions do they have?

10 What would they do if they woke up and heard a strange noise in their home?

Now answer these questions for another major character.

Are these two characters' routine lives sufficiently different from each other to make them realistic individuals in the world of the story you have created?

Making choices

Whether we recognize it or not, we have choices about everything we do. However, once we have worked out the best way to do something, it would be a waste of time to consider these choices every time we do it. We therefore create routine ways of behaving when we perform tasks repeatedly, so that we barely need to put any conscious thought into.

Consider the number of things you do routinely every day: get up, shower, get dressed, eat breakfast, clean your teeth, work, eat lunch, etc. What other activities do you repeat less frequently? Putting out the bins? Taking the kids to football practice? Having your hair cut? Cleaning the car? Visiting relatives? Celebrating religious festivals or other events?

Although we put very little conscious thought into much of what we do, our subconscious mind gives us a myriad instructions for performing even the most routine tasks and what choices to make when we do it. Think for a moment how many actions are involved in washing your hair. Just picking up the shampoo bottle involves:

▶ stretching your arm out to just the right place to reach the bottle

▶ stretching out your fingers the right amount to surround the bottle

▶ closing your fingers around the bottle

▶ applying just the right pressure to pick up the bottle

▶ moving your arm back so the bottle is in the desired position.

Although you are unlikely to even notice it, each time you carry out the most simple routines, you make choices by tapping into your memories, beliefs, values, thinking patterns and even the state you are in. For example, washing your hair requires:

▶ memories that include:

  ▷ how you've successfully washed your hair in the past

  ▷ how you've unsuccessfully washed your hair in the past

▶ beliefs that are likely to include:

  ▷ that your hair is dirty enough to need a wash

  ▷ what you need to do to make your hair clean

  ▷ how you know that your hair is clean

▶ values: at some level you believe it is important to have clean hair. Maybe you value:

  ▷ health, and see hair hygiene as contributing to this

  ▷ appearance

  ▷ fitting in

  ▷ some other value

- thinking patterns: many different patterns could be at work when you wash your hair, for example:

  ▷ perhaps you desire to impress someone with your clean hair and are operating a Towards style of thinking

  ▷ perhaps you don't want people to think badly of you for having dirty hair and are operating an Away From thinking style.

Your state will also impact on how you wash your hair. For example:

- if you're running late, you may hurry the process
- if you're sleepy, you may take it slowly.

Strategies

NLP refers to the thought processes that lead us through our routines and habitual behaviours as **strategies**. NLP also considers the thought processes that lead us through new challenges and any deviations from our routines as strategies. Our beliefs, values, thinking patterns, memories and the state we are in influence the choices involved in even our most basic routines, and therefore they also influence the thought process NLP calls a strategy.

Key idea

A *strategy* is the thought process that leads us through the way we do something and informs us about which choices to make.

Strategies are learned using three basic methods:

- observing, experiencing or being taught the way someone else does something and doing it that way yourself; NLP refers to this as **modelling**
- testing if a certain way of doing something works
- a mixture of using what we have learned from observation/ experience/teaching and testing what works.

We can't remember learning many of the everyday strategies we use, because we learned them from watching or taking part in experiences in our childhood. For example, you probably learned to wash your hair by observing and experiencing whoever cared for you as a child washing your hair. You will also have learned to wash your hair partly by testing; for example, how tightly to close your eyes or how far to tip your head back so that the shampoo doesn't run into them and sting them.

The strategies we use in many everyday situations are therefore a product of our upbringing. If we want our characters to be recognized as real people, many of their habitual strategies also need to be a product of their upbringing. This idea again highlights the importance of understanding our characters' backgrounds, because different cultures, different religions, different societies, different parts of society and simply different people do things differently.

Presupposition: Everyone lives in their own unique model of the world.

The differences in our upbringing lead to people having different routine strategies for achieving the same thing. This can vary from such obvious differences as one person heating baked beans in the microwave while another heats them in a pan on the hob, to internal invisible strategies, such a person with a good memory having a better memory strategy than someone with a poor memory.

Try it now

Consider the customs, traditions and rituals that you were exposed to in your upbringing.

* Did you learn specific cultural or religious traditions and rituals?
* How did your family add their own variations to these traditions and rituals?
* What family traditions did you have?
* Did you have any particular 'job' or 'role' as child within your family traditions?
* In what routine ways were you expected to behave? For example, what manners were you taught, what chores were you expected to do?

Routine strategies and character

If they are culture- specific, the most mundane activities can tell us about the world a character comes from. Even the simplest things, like how they make a cup of tea – indeed, whether they know how to make a cup of tea – can tell us (and our audience) about them and their history. Some routines and automatic reactions and behaviours in everyday situations can also give away the beliefs and values planted in their past; for example, crossing yourself when in danger if you're a Roman Catholic.

Try it now

Reconsider the answers you gave to the questions in the self-assessment at the start of this chapter for one of your characters. What do your answers tell you about:

* ✳ what they believe?
* ✳ what's important to them?
* ✳ their values?
* ✳ their past experiences?
* ✳ how they think?

Note: You may already have some answers to these questions from working through Chapters 1–3 and/or from any other work you have done.

Key idea

Every character's upbringing has a huge impact on the way they perform even the most ordinary tasks and activities. Asking ourselves how a character does something or deals with everyday/routine occurrences can tell us a lot about their past and 'where they've come from'.

UNUSUAL ROUTINES

Sometimes it can be advantageous to write characters who have unusual 'everyday' routines, interesting rituals or superstitions, or carry out everyday tasks in an unusual way. This adds to their sense of character and stimulates our audience's curiosity about their past, who they are and how they tackle the rest of their lives.

These interesting strategies can also make characters more memorable. However, it's important to ensure that any unusual strategies are congruent with who a character is and that the unusual behaviour isn't so unusual that it appears ridiculous – unless, of course, you want it to appear ridiculous.

CONNECTING WITH OUR AUDIENCE

As well as establishing our characters' backgrounds and who they are, routine strategies can be used to build connections with our audience when we are writing about a character they might find it difficult to connect with.

Carrying out a commonplace routine can demonstrate to our audience that a character is just like them. For example, seeing an alien kiss his kids goodbye and head out to work, or a 17th-century man drinking with his friends, triggers a subconscious recognition that they are like us, if we do those things. It's also worth remembering that something that is an alien experience to our audience can be something very usual in the 'real world', such as being an air traffic controller.

Remember this

Although showing characters' routines can be useful, make sure you don't bore your audience with the minutiae of their lives. Always ensure any everyday routines work within the plot and that you aren't just showing a character's routine strategy for the sake of it.

When characters need new strategies

NLP considers that the **TOTE model** is the basic pattern that all strategies fit into. Tote stands for:

1 Test

2 Operation

3 Test

4 Exit

The TOTE process is kicked off when we recognize that we want to achieve something.

- ▶ **Test** means we compare where we are now with what we want to achieve.

- ▶ **Operation** is the actions we take to reduce the difference between where we are now and what we want to achieve.

- ▶ The second **Test** is when we compare whether the action we have taken has reduced the difference between where we are and what we want to achieve.

- ▶ **Exit** is when there is no difference between where we are and what we want to achieve, i.e. we have achieved what we want to achieve.

NLP considers that we go through the TOTE process every time we carry out a strategy. As we grow up, we build up a huge collection of strategies that help us to navigate our world (through the TOTE process) without putting much conscious thought into the vast majority of activities. We also fail to notice that we are making choices and have a choice about what we do when we carry out routine strategies. We therefore act almost on autopilot as we work through them.

The implication of this for our characters is that while they are in their world and their world is reacting in the way they expect it to, they will continue to act in line with the strategies they have learned, barely thinking about the choices they are making. It is only when they are thrown out of their world, their world changes or new challenges arise that they think harder about the strategies they operate and recognize that they have choices. It is at such points that the TOTE process becomes more visible.

Case study

In the 1997 film *Titanic*, a third-class passenger, Jack Dawson, is invited to a first-class table for dinner. Jack is entering a social world that he is unfamiliar with and is at high risk of making a fool of himself, particularly as two of the characters at the table are keen to impress his 'lack of class' on him. Jack, unsurprisingly, wants to retain his dignity and is also keen to develop his relationship with Rose DeWitt Bukater, who is at the table, and win her affection. He therefore needs to fit in with the 'first-class world' and 'look good' in front of Rose.

If Jack is to achieve these outcomes in this unfamiliar world, he has to think actively about how to deal with the new situations he encounters. His TOTE processes therefore become more visible than when he is working through strategies he has already learned.

For example, Jack slouches against a pillar as he waits for Rose to arrive. However, he observes another man standing upright with one hand behind his back. Jack recognizes that he can make a 'better' choice about how to stand and strikes this pose to make himself fit in. The TOTE process that is kicked off by Jack's desire to fit in and appear as the other men do is:

* **Test**: Jack compares his posture (slouching) with the other man's posture (standing upright with one hand behind his back).
* **Operation**: Jack assumes the posture of the other man.
* **Test**: Jack compares his posture with the other man's posture.
* **Exit**: Jack's posture is the same as the other man's.

Jack continues to navigate the dinner by operating a fresh TOTE for each unfamiliar situation and occurrence.

Remember this

Not all of the characters in a story will necessarily encounter new challenges. Furthermore, some may remain on autopilot – or near autopilot – despite facing new challenges. This in itself tells us something about these characters.

TOTES WITHIN TOTES

The TOTE framework can be applied to challenges of any size. For example, the TOTE model can be used to describe Jack's strategy to stand correctly as he waits for Rose and his strategy to navigate the whole dinner.

How a character addresses the new challenges they face shows our audience a huge amount about who a character is. As we saw earlier, a character's memories, values, thinking patterns and beliefs – which include the strategies they have already learned – and their state will all impact on how they tackle the routine choices they face. These influences also dictate how characters deal with new challenges they recognise, and indeed whether they deal with new challenges or run away from them.

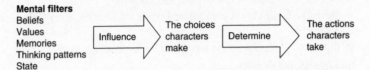

Mental filters
Beliefs
Values
Memories
Thinking patterns
State

Because stories are about growth and learning, at least one of our main characters needs to find themselves in new situations where they have to create new strategies or remould old ones. This is why stories require an inciting incident. The inciting incident takes our main character(s) off autopilot and makes them think about the choices they have.

Considering a character's approach within the TOTE model when they face challenges and new situations is, therefore, another way we can explore who they are and/or show our audience who that character is and how they feel.

Case study

Returning to the film *Titanic*, we can explore Jack's approach to navigating the first-class dinner – which is basically to think on his feet – and see what it might tell us about his beliefs, values, memories, thinking patterns and state.

If we consider Jack navigating the whole dinner as a single TOTE, we see that Jack thinking on his feet describes the operation stage.

Choosing to think on his feet suggests that Jack:

* has experience of succeeding by living by his wits
* has confidence in himself and his abilities. This confidence will be based on his beliefs, which might include beliefs about his intelligence, luck, equality.
* has values that are satisfied by this way of operating. These might include self-reliance, intelligence, risk and adventure.
* is framing the situation as a challenge that he is sufficiently equipped to deal with.

Jack will be in a state of 'high alert' as he thinks on his feet and works hard to achieve his desired outcomes. His thinking styles (and therefore the styles he probably usually operates) are:

* Best-Case Scenario – expecting the best outcome
* Towards – looking for how to succeed rather than running away from a situation
* Big Chunk – focusing on the bigger picture and dealing with the minutiae as they arise
* Other – being aware of and responding well to other people's reactions and non-verbal signals.

We also see that Jack:

* learns a lot by observation – this is congruent with his character being a talented artist
* learns from Rose's unspoken direction – demonstrating the bond and the trust that has already grown between them
* works hard to get it right – demonstrating that he is modest enough to think he might fail and that it is important to him to succeed.

If we consider this case study further, we can see that thinking on his feet was not the only way Jack could have acted in the operation stage. Jack could have:

▶ asked someone to talk him through what would happen at the dinner and the relevant etiquettes, then repeated them at the right time

▶ found out what was on the menu and asked someone to teach him how to tackle each course.

There are probably several other approaches Jack could have taken to navigating the dinner. Furthermore, he could have decided to achieve a completely different outcome when faced with the invitation to dinner, such as accepting that he was not well bred enough to pursue Rose. His action then might have been not to attend the dinner at all. If he had done this, it would have told us very different things about Jack – see Chapters 1, 2 and 3 for further discussion of the way beliefs, values and thinking patterns impact on the goals we aim for.

Key idea

The strategies our characters choose to pursue and the approaches they take to creating new strategies tell us and our audience about who that character is, how they feel and how they are thinking.

EXPLORING YOUR OWN CHARACTERS

When we, as the author of our story, consider the Operation stage of the TOTE process, we make choices on behalf of our characters about how to achieve their desired outcome(s). If we take time at this stage to consider all the possible options available, we can identify which one(s) the character in question is most likely to be drawn towards taking. This allows us to ensure there is congruity between who the character is and the actions they take.

Alternatively, if we are the sort of writer who considers plot before character, or moves between developing plot and character, we can choose the option(s) we want a character to choose or think a character would choose and explore these to identify more information about who that character is.

Try it now

TOTE a challenge that a character faces in your work in progress. Consider what actions they take at the Operation stage. If you are undecided about what they would choose to do, choose, one possible set of actions they could take.

What do the actions they choose tell you about:
* the strategies the character has used in the past?
* the beliefs the character holds?
* the confidence the character has in themselves?
* the values that are satisfied by this option and therefore might be important to the character?
* the way they frame the situation?
* the thinking styles the character is operating?
* the character's state?
Is there anything else you learn?

Using the exercise above can help you to examine:

▶ a character who isn't fully developed and what making different choices would expose about that character's beliefs, values, thinking patterns, memories and state

▶ whether there is more than one set of actions a character can take and still maintain congruence with who they are.

▶ whether an already well-developed character will be acting 'in character' by taking the option(s) they choose. If the options they choose make them act out of character, you can consider:

▷ what different actions they might choose

▷ how you could manipulate your character to perform the chosen operation(s) while remaining true to themselves (see also Chapter 4)

Remember this

We can explore our characters by thinking about what they have experienced and learned in the past and predicting the actions this will lead them to take. Alternatively, we can look at the actions a character takes and ask what these actions tell us about them.

Focus points

The main points to remember from this chapter are:

✳ A strategy is the thought process that leads us through the way we do something.

✳ Every strategy a character carries out is influenced by their beliefs, values, thinking patterns, memories and state.

✳ Every character's upbringing has a huge impact on the way they perform even the most mundane tasks and activities.

✳ NLP considers TOTE to be the basic strategy pattern that all strategies fit into.

✳ The strategies our characters use reveal information about their past, who they are and how they are thinking.

Next step

In Chapter 6, we will explore NLP's concepts of deletion, distortion and generalization. We will see how people use these processes to deal with the huge amount of information the world throws at them and with the information they share. We will also explore how beliefs, values, thinking patterns and state influence what people delete, distort and generalize, and how an understanding of these processes can improve characterization and storytelling.

Part 2

Getting inside your characters'
and your audience's heads

6

Truth, lies and everything in between

In this chapter you will learn about:

▶ *the concepts of deletion, distortion and generalization*

▶ *how deletion, distortion and generalization influence people's experiences and their individuality*

▶ *how deletion, distortion and generalization impact on our writing*

▶ *how deletion, distortion and generalization can be used to improve our storytelling.*

Self-assessment: Are you getting far enough inside your characters' heads?

Without reading this diagnostic test any further, rewrite the first page of your work in progress from the point of view of a different character from the one you have used. If only one character is in the scene on the first page, rewrite the first page of your story that has more than one character on it.

Now read through both your original first page and the one you have just created. What information, if any, does this second point of view reveal that the first didn't? Does either point of view contradict the other?

1 If both characters revealed exactly the same information, you are probably not thinking deeply enough about who your characters are and/or developing their perspective adequately.

2 If there were differences in the information the characters revealed – beyond any differences caused by where they are physically placed – then you have been considering who they are and how they process the world.

3 If your characters have twisted events to fit their own agenda or view of the world, either intentionally or unintentionally, you are working strongly with how different people process the world around them.

Seeing what we want to see

Chapters 1–5 considered the filters we use to understand and deal with the situations we find ourselves in. However, this is not the whole story about how we deal with our experiences.

The world throws a huge amount of information at us through our five senses. However, our brains are only able to process a certain amount of this information at any one time. In 1956, the American psychologist George A. Miller identified that our conscious mind can normally hold seven items of information (plus or minus two) at any given time. If we held more, our conscious mind couldn't cope with so much information. However, many people can't handle even this number.

DEALING WITH WHAT THE WORLD THROWS AT US

If you stop and look around next time you are walking through your local town, you will notice how much can be going on around you that you aren't consciously aware of. This is because our brains stop us becoming overloaded with input by **deleting, distorting** and **generalizing** the incoming information. We also use deletion, distortion and generalization, both intentionally and unintentionally, when we share information with others.

▶ Deletion

Deletion occurs when we focus selectively, either consciously or subconsciously, on certain aspects of our experience and not others. We then overlook or omit details we aren't paying attention to or don't think important. If you've ever told someone something only for them to deny, in all sincerity, that you ever said it some time later, you will have experienced someone using deletion. This does not mean they intentionally ignored you but that their brain was giving higher priority to something else.

Deletion isn't intrinsically good or bad. It can be positive, for example, when we're working in a busy environment and need to filter out noise in order to concentrate. Negative examples include when we delete a piece of information that later turns out to be more important than we realized or stepping out in front of a car because we were too focused on talking on our mobile phone while crossing the road.

▶ Distortion

Distortion can occur in different ways and can also happen both intentionally or unintentionally.

▶ We may focus on certain aspects of an experience and distort them to be more or less important than others. For example, if we have low self-esteem we may see our contribution to a team game as less important that it really was. If we are overly confident, we may think we were instrumental in winning the game when in fact we were a liability to our team.

- We can imagine things to be physically bigger or smaller than they really are. If you have ever returned as an adult to your first school, you will probably have been surprised at how small it was. This is one example of how experience is distorted by our perspective; in this case we hold a distorted memory of the school as being much larger than it was because at the time we were so small.

- Distortion includes making assumptions and jumping to conclusions. For example, if we are in a good mood we may assume someone smiles at us because they like us. However, if we have an embarrassing secret to hide, we may conclude that they are laughing at us.

- Distortion also includes altering the sequence of events or adding things that weren't even there or that didn't happen.

- We may also distort time, remembering things as happening more quickly or more slowly than they did.

Like deletion, distortion can have both negative and positive impacts. Furthermore, it can also be a creative process, such as when we fantasize, daydream, develop inventions, imagine ourselves in other people's shoes, tell jokes and, of course, when we make up stories.

▶ Generalization

Generalization allows us to predict the world by taking one example and using it to represent a whole group. For example, if we eat something we don't like the taste of, we will generalize that the same thing will taste the same if we it eat again. This stops us repeating unpleasant experiences. If we have a good experience, we will generalize that the experience will be good again and be happy to repeat it. Generalization also stops us having to keep working out how to do things over and over again. For example, once we have learned how to drive one car, we can use the model of how to drive, which we have created in our heads, to drive a different car.

Generalization can also have negative and positive consequences. If we are bitten by a dog, we may generalize that all dogs are dangerous. This may lead us to be cautious around dogs, but if taken to an extreme we may develop a phobia of dogs.

SHARING OUR EXPERIENCES

Deletion, distortion and generalization are not just part of our process of interpreting and storing incoming information. We also delete, distort and generalize when we share information, such as:

▶ missing out details we think unimportant

▶ generalizing ideas to fit our models of the way we think things are

▶ distorting events by playing up the parts we think most important

▶ distorting events by missing out what we think is unimportant.

If we didn't delete, distort and generalize, it would take all day to explain even the smallest things. Deletion, distortion and generalization also give us the ability to manipulate the information we give to people and influence the way they see things.

Key idea

Our brains subconsciously *delete*, *distort* and *generalize* incoming information in order to avoid becoming overloaded. However, we also both consciously and subconsciously delete, distort and generalize when we are sharing information or experiences with others.

Deletion, distortion and generalization aren't good or bad in themselves; they are our way of coping with the information we take in and how we share it with others. They can have a positive, negative or neutral impact on ourselves and/or those around us.

Try it now

Consider your work in progress. Identify some deletions, distortions or generalizations your main characters make that are demonstrated by what they say and/or the way they behave in the story. If you are struggling to recognize any, try reading the first chapter or first few scenes and identifying some. Also, remember that fears, phobias, assumptions and prejudices all demonstrate generalization and/or distortion.

Presupposition: Everyone lives in their own unique model of the world.

When two people have the same experience, they don't necessarily create the same memory of that experience. For example, one small child may tell you that they met a big, fluffy dog in the park, another child may meet the same dog and say they saw a huge, ferocious beast. One mother may tell you the dog was small and smooth-coated, while the other may not even remember seeing a dog.

The differences in what we perceive and remember arise because people don't all delete, distort or generalize in the same way. We delete, distort and generalize incoming and outgoing information based on the filters discussed in Chapters 1–4: beliefs, values, memories, thinking patterns and state. Since these filters are unique to us, we delete, distort and generalize in our own unique ways. Our deletions, distortions and generalizations then impact in turn on our beliefs, values, memories, thinking patterns and state, either reinforcing them or changing them in some way.

Experience

↓

Deletion, distortion and generalization
of the experience
determined by our
beliefs, values, memories, thinking patterns and state

↓

Interpretation of experience

↓

Beliefs, values, memories, thinking patterns and state
reinforced, modified or created
by our interpretation of the experience

Remember this

Because we are all unique, two people may encounter exactly the same experience but perceive and interpret it completely differently.

Seeing more clearly, writing more thoughtfully

Once we understand deletion, distortion and generalization, we can use this understanding to:

▶ ensure our characters act consistently and convincingly

▶ improve our understanding of what we are writing about

▶ improve our storytelling

▶ influence our audience

▶ create bonds between characters (see 'How do people create rapport? in Chapter 10).

ENSURING OUR CHARACTERS ACT CONSISTENTLY AND CONVINCINGLY

Our audience is highly unlikely to think in terms of what deletions, distortions and generalizations our characters are making. However, they are likely to notice if characters delete, distort or generalize in a way inappropriate to who they are or the situation or state they are in.

To understand how a character is likely to delete, distort or generalize, or to check if their deletions, distortions and generalizations in a given situation are congruent with their beliefs, values, memories, state and habitual thinking patterns, consider the following.

▶ What would their beliefs, values, memories, state and habitual thinking patterns tell them is important about the situation? (Your character is likely to distort these things to increase their importance and focus on them more strongly.)

▶ What would their beliefs, values, memories, state and habitual thinking patterns tell them is unimportant about the situation? (Your character is likely to delete or reduce the importance of these things in their thinking and/or when they are talking about them.)

▶ How would they generalize their experience to fit the models they already have of the way things are?

▶ Would what they are experiencing confront any beliefs, values, memories, state or habitual thinking patterns sufficiently to make them remould these and consequently delete, distort or generalize differently to the way they have previously?

IMPROVING YOUR UNDERSTANDING OF WHAT YOU ARE WRITING ABOUT

Because deletion, distortion and generalization filter our experiences and influence our memories of them, writers need to consider the impact of deletion, distortion and generalization on experiences they are calling upon when they write. This applies equally whether we are calling upon information in our memories or researching new ideas and information.

▶ Deletion

Because deletion cuts out what we consider to be irrelevant or what we don't want to acknowledge, writing from memory can mean we miss out details that it might be important to include. Reliving an experience or revisiting a place we are writing about can help us to discover details that we have previously deleted when creating our memories.

When Helen Peters was writing her children's novel *The Secret Hen House Theatre*, she returned to the farm where she had lived as a child and was amazed by the new information she gained.

'When I was redrafting, I visited the farm every month for a year,' says Helen, 'notebook in hand, recording sensory details. It was amazing how much more I noticed this way. I knew the yard was muddy in winter, of course, but I'd never noticed that the mud was printed all over with the spiky footprints of chickens.'

Here Helen is recognizing that she has previously deleted memories of the chickens' footprints in the mud, presumably because when she saw them as a child they were of no importance to her.

Remember this

Sometimes the most familiar places are the most important for us to revisit, because we tend to delete the familiar more easily.

When we are researching, we may also ignore facts that don't fit our plot or don't seem relevant or exciting. This isn't a problem unless we then end up glossing over or ignoring facts that don't suit us and so cause inconsistencies or errors in our work.

▶ Distortion

Reliving an experience or revisiting a place we are writing about can also help us to identify things we have distorted in our memories. However, sometimes we might continue to apply a distortion. For example, if we are afraid of water, a boat trip is likely to remain a scary experience if we revisit it.

To help counterbalance this sort of distortion, consider how your own personal feelings, beliefs, values, memories, thinking patterns and emotions might impact on a place or an experience before you relive it. This may help you to identify distortions you might have applied and be wary of applying them when you revisit. If you think you may not be able to step outside the distortion when you revisit, taking a friend with you or asking others to share their memories of a place or experience can also help to identify the personal distortions you have applied. However, remember that other people may be applying their own distortions, deletions and generalizations too.

▶ Generalization

On the one hand, generalization allows us to extrapolate useful ideas from a small amount of research, but on the other hand, it can lead us to do insufficient research. For example, we don't have to visit every 15th-century church in England to make sure that we create a historically accurate description of a fictitious 15th-century church. However, if we are writing about a specific 15th-century English church, it wouldn't be safe to assume that it's the same as all the other 15th-century English churches we have seen.

Generalization can also lead us to apply a distortion we have created to similar new experiences.

Try it now

Chose a place from your childhood that you can visit easily and that you were familiar with but rarely visit now.

Engaging all your senses – sight, hearing, feeling, taste and smell – write a description of this place.

Now go to the place and observe as much detail as you can, once more engaging all your senses. What did you delete, distort and/or generalize in the first description you wrote?

Next consider your own feelings, beliefs, values and memories. Could any of these lead you to feel particular emotions that distort the way you see this place now?

Key idea

Ensure you research and observe details and facts as fully and as dispassionately as is possible and practicable.

IMPROVING YOUR STORYTELLING AND INFLUENCING YOUR AUDIENCE

As we have learned in Chapters 1–4, everyone's mental filtering system is unique, and this uniqueness means that how we delete, distort and generalize is unique to each person. As well as influencing the memories we create, deletion, distortion and generalization also filter outgoing information. What information we share and how we share it with our audience has a huge impact on the final story we produce.

▶ 1 Detail

Once you have explored a place or an experience fully, it can be tempting to share everything with your audience. However, your audience will only be able to retain so much of what you tell them. Too many details or facts can make the most interesting story boring or give the impression that you're trying to educate rather than entertain. It's also important not to meander off on anecdotes or stories that take your audience up blind alleyways just because you found them interesting or exciting when you researched or experienced them.

When you are writing prose, always ensure the facts and sensory descriptions you share create an image, atmosphere or understanding rather than boring or overwhelming your audience. Place details and facts sparingly, so that the story flows naturally and they sit almost invisibly within it: give a 'flavour' rather than entire recipe. Your audience will fill in the blanks with their imagination.

Try it now

Consider the place you visited in the previous exercise. What are the five single details that together give the strongest impression of it?

Prose writers

Write a description of someone walking through this place for the first time using only these five details to describe it.

Scriptwriters

Imagine someone walking through this place for the first time focusing only on these five details.

The chances are there's little, if anything, more that you need to add to create a strong impression in your audience's mind.

Repeat the exercise using only the three most important details. Did you really need five?

Note: Chapter 8 discusses sharing details with your audience in greater depth.

▶ 2 Exposition

If you need to include a large amount of factual information, back-story or revelation, don't dump it all into your story at once. This will overwhelm your audience, your work will seem less interesting, and it will be easier for your audience to forget what you tell them. Spread factual information, back-story or revelation through your work and weigh up what is and isn't truly essential.

It's also important to remember that our audience also deletes, distorts and generalizes the information they receive through their own personal filters. This means that we need to:

▶ give sufficient exposure to what it is important for them to know and understand

▶ recognize that certain images and ideas can lead people of a similar background or with similar experiences to distort or generalize in a certain ways.

Try it now

What assumptions would you usually make about:

✳ a man wearing a hoodie who has a squat, muscular dog?
✳ a child with holes in their shoes?
✳ the location of a block of flats in serious disrepair?
✳ the location of a pretty thatched cottage?
✳ a strange man you find standing at the foot of your bed in the middle of the night?

Now ask your partner or best friend what assumptions they would usually make.

What do your cultural similarities and/or differences lead you and your partner/friend to assume?

Distortions and generalizations are usually context and/or culture specific. For example, in a ghost story your audience is likely to assume that the man standing at the foot of the protagonist's bed is a ghost. In crime fiction, they are likely to assume him a criminal.

▶ 3 Point of view

Each character in our story will delete, distort and generalize as they take in and impart information to the audience and to one another. What they change and how will be different for every character. For example, a 10-year-old whose only experience of war is from films and television will see and talk about war in a very different way from an 80-year-old war veteran. Understanding your character's perspective is therefore vital to understanding the deletions, distortions and generalizations they are likely to make.

How a character deletes, distorts and generalizes can also be critical in choosing which character to make the 'point-of-view' character in our writing, because whoever we choose will be in control of the information our audience receives. They will, either intentionally or unintentionally, share, hold back, distort or generalize what 'they' tell the audience.

Chapter 13 shows some ways of exploring which are the right character(s) to tell a story. However, when considering who should deliver the majority viewpoint in your story, you may also find it useful to consider what information you wish to hide or reveal and when you may wish to conceal or reveal it.

Writers themselves can also decide what deletions, distortions and generalizations to make within a piece of work, and to some extent all writers chose a perspective from which to show their work – even documentary film-makers choose a point of view and slant the information they share accordingly. We shall explore this idea further in 'Twists and surprises' below.

Key idea

Our characters(s) delete, distort and generalize the information they take in and share with one another and with the audience. Always ensure you apply to a character's perspective the deletions, distortions and generalizations that they would be likely to make and **not** the deletions, distortions and generalizations that you would make.

The 'unreliable narrator'

In reality, all narrators are unreliable because we all have a unique view of the world and delete, distort and generalize accordingly, disseminating information based on our personal perspective. However, 'unreliable narrator' is a literary term applied to stories told from a first person point of view in which what the narrator tells the audience is intended to be perceived at some stage by the audience as biased or untrustworthy.

Typical reasons for a narrator being unreliable include that:

▶ the narrator holds prejudices

▶ the narrator is a child putting their interpretation on adult events

▶ the narrator suffers from mental illness or dementia

▶ the narrator has a personality flaw, such as pathological lying or narcissism

▶ the narrator has some form of agenda and wants to persuade their audience to think a certain way.

Whatever the reason for the narrator being an unreliable narrator, at some point the audience will realize that his or her interpretation of events cannot be fully trusted and will begin to form their own opinions about the events and motivations within the story.

If you chose to use an unreliable narrator, you will need to be more than usually aware of the difference between what your 'point-of-view' character is telling your audience and what else you want your audience to deduce about them. Considering how, what and why your character deletes, distorts and generalizes incoming and outgoing information can help you to differentiate their version of events from the 'reality' you wish to show to your audience.

Twists and surprises

A writer may want it to be clear to their audience from early in the story that they are engaging with an unreliable narrator. However, some stories use an unreliable narrator to introduce a twist or surprise by suddenly revealing some way into the story that the narrator is unreliable.

Twists and surprises can also be created in film without the use of an unreliable narrator – although here the camera could be considered the unreliable narrator – by exploiting the tendency of similar cultures to make similar deletions, distortions and generalizations and manipulating the audience into drawing particular conclusions that aren't 'true'. The audience is then surprised when the story reveals the 'truth'.

Case study

The 1999 film *The Sixth Sense* tells the story of Cole Sears, a troubled boy who can talk to the dead, and a child psychologist, Dr Malcolm Crowe, who tries to help him. Most audiences were surprised to discover at the end of the film that Dr Crowe is a ghost by the first time he meets Cole. Yet on watching the film again, they saw many clues telling them that he was dead. This happened because the director used techniques exploiting the likelihood that people would delete, distort and generalize in certain ways. Here are some of them:

Distortion

* At the beginning of the film we see Crowe being shot, followed by a scene subtitled 'The next fall'. That scene shows Crowe sitting on a bench watching Cole. We assume Crowe survived the gunshot because we haven't seen him die or his funeral.

* In one scene we see Crowe sitting opposite Cole's mother as they wait for Cole to arrive home from school. We assume they've been talking to each other. As Cole's mother leaves, she says, 'You've got an hour', meaning an hour until their meal time, but we assume she means Cole has an hour with Dr Crowe.

* After Cole is involved in a confrontation at school, the next scene shows Crowe and Cole sitting in a headmaster's type office. We assume the school has called Crowe in.

Deletion

* We delete the unusual situation that after Dr Crowe is shot at the start of the film, he never has a proper conversation with anyone but Cole.

Generalization

* When Crowe is late for their anniversary dinner, his wife ignores him, because he's a ghost. As people do behave like this when they're angry with someone, we assume that's why she's ignoring him.

* Cole is afraid of all the other ghosts, so we assume he is afraid of all ghosts.

Remember this

Writers can intentionally delete, distort and generalize to give their audience the experience(s) they want them to have.

4 Stereotypes

Because generalization leads us to develop certain frames which we apply to particular people, places and experiences, we often hold stereotypes in our heads. When you considered the assumptions you made about certain people and places in the earlier exercise in this chapter, it is likely to have led you to identify some stereotypes. Did you see:

▶ the man wearing a hoodie who has a squat, muscular dog as aggressive or confrontational?

▶ the child with holes in their shoes as coming from a poor family or as neglected?

▶ the block of flats in serious disrepair as located in an inner-city area?

▶ the pretty thatched cottage as located in the countryside?

Placing generalizations in a story can save time and explanation. However, it's important to be aware that generalization can lead to cliché, two-dimensional characters, boring your audience and churning out stories that lack originality and life. Don't allow your own generalization to short-circuit your imagination. Don't just grab the nearest idea, setting, character or phrase that works for the story you're writing. Take time to move away from generalizations – not all pirates wear eyepatches, not all models are anorexic, not all scientists are mad, not all aliens want to take over the planet....

Breaking stereotypes can also challenge your audience's generalizations and make them think harder. However it's important to remember that some audiences don't want to think, let alone think hard. Whether you choose to challenge them is, of course, up to you.

Focus points

The main points to remember from this chapter are:

✳ Our brains subconsciously delete, distort and generalize incoming information in order to make sense of the world.

✳ People also consciously and subconsciously delete, distort and generalize when they share information or experiences with others.

* Deletion, distortion and generalization aren't good or bad in themselves; they are our way of coping with the information we take in and how we share it with others. Deletion, distortion and generalization can have a positive, negative or neutral impact on ourselves and those around us.

* People delete, distort and generalize incoming information based on their mental filters, which act largely subconsciously. These filters are beliefs, values, memories, thinking patterns and the state we are in.

* Narrator(s) and characters also delete, distort and generalize the information they take in and what they share with one another and with your audience. The audience will then delete, distort and generalize that information using their own filters. We can use this both to characterize and to manipulate our audience's perceptions.

Next step

In Chapter 7, we will consider how we take in information through our five senses. We will explore the idea that most people have a dominant sense, which impacts on their understanding of the stories we tell. We will use this understanding to explore how to engage our audience more effectively and also consider the importance of our characters' having a dominant sense.

7

Memory, understanding and imagination

In this chapter you will learn about:

- ▶ *the concept of representational systems*
- ▶ *how people's representational systems can affect the way they perceive and engage with our stories*
- ▶ *how understanding representational systems can help writers connect more strongly with their audiences*
- ▶ *how a character's upbringing can influence their representational systems.*

Self-assessment: Identifying your primary representational system

Consider the following questions and note down whether you answer a, b or c. If you cannot decide between two choices, note down both letters.

1 When you create a new character, do you tend to focus first on:

   a how they look or dress?

   b how they talk and what they say?

   c who they are/what they believe/how they feel?

2 What do you dislike most when you read a piece of fiction, apart from poor writing in general or a genre you don't enjoy?

   a Insufficient or poor description

   b Dialogue that doesn't feel genuine

   c Not fully experiencing what the character is doing or feeling

3 If you take some time off, what do you prefer to do?

   a See a play or film or visit an art gallery, historic building, garden or museum

   b Go to a concert/listen to music

   c Spend time with friends or take part in a physical activity, such as dancing or sport

4 When you are being taught something new, do you prefer initially:

   a to be shown pictures, diagrams and/or be given written explanations?

   b to listen to what is being said and discuss it?

   c to have a go for yourself by putting what is being taught into practice?

5 When you need to find a solution to a challenge in your writing, do you:

   a picture how your characters make their way through it?

   b discuss possible solutions in your head or listen to your characters talk about it?

c fiddle with things, go for a walk or chew your pen as you work out what to do?

6 When you feel especially connected to a character you are writing, is it because of:

a how they look?

b what they say to you?

c how you feel about them?

7 When you go to a live music performance, do you get the most out of:

a the musician's image and watching them perform?

b listening to the lyrics and music?

c dancing/moving in time with the music and/or the way it makes you feel?

8 When you research a piece of writing, do you prefer to:

a look at books/search the Internet?

b talk to people?

c have a go at experiencing what you're researching?

9 Consider your favourite word, if you have one, or the type of words you enjoy using most. Do you like it/them because of:

a the way they look when written down?

b the sound they make when spoken?

c the feeling they give you?

10 When you 'people watch', what do you notice first?

a How they look or dress

b What they say or how they sound

c How you feel about them or what they are doing.

You will be asked to reflect on your answers to these questions later in this chapter.

Representational systems

We perceive the world through our five senses, which NLP refers to as **modalities**. However, we don't just use sight, sound, feeling, taste and smell to take in our surroundings. We also use our senses to recreate memories and to imagine experiences that haven't happened to us, people we haven't met and places we haven't visited.

When our brain uses one of our senses to recreate real or imagined events, it is described by NLP as using a **representational system**. For example, when we visualize something, we are considered to be using our visual representational system.

The five representational systems are often referred to in NLP by the acronym **VAKOG**, which stands for: Visual (seeing), Auditory (hearing), Kinaesthetic (feeling and touching), Olfactory (smell), Gustatory (taste).

Key idea

When our brain uses one of our senses to recreate real or imagined events it is described by NLP as using a *representational system*.

PRIMARY REPRESENTATIONAL SYSTEMS

Unless we have a physical inability to perceive a particular sense, we all learn, perceive and recreate the world through all our senses and our feelings. However, most people tend to favour one sense. This is called their primary or preferred representational system. Most people also tend to favour either their visual, auditory or kinaesthetic system.

▶ **Visual**

If we have a visual preference, we predominantly perceive things visually and take notice of images more strongly than the information supplied by our other senses. When we remember or recreate experiences in our mind or imagine new ones, we primarily see pictures of those experiences.

▶ **Auditory**

People with an auditory preference take more notice of sound: voices, noises, music. When they remember or use their imaginations, they do this largely by imagining sounds and talking to themselves, either inside their heads or out loud.

▶ Kinaesthetic

The kinaesthetic system is considered to include touch, feelings and physical experience. A kinaesthetic preference predominantly manifests itself in our memories and imagination as sensations of touch, movement and the way we feel emotionally about something.

▶ Olfactory and Gustatory

The olfactory representational system recreates smells and the gustatory system recreates tastes. Although these representational systems are usually less well-developed, they do operate as the primary systems in some people.

IDENTIFYING YOUR PRIMARY REPRESENTATIONAL SYSTEM

The questions you answered at the start of this chapter were designed to help you recognize which representational system or systems you favour.

If you answered mostly:

a you are likely to favour your visual system

b you are likely to favour your auditory system

c you are likely to favour your kinaesthetic system.

If your answers consist of equal, or roughly equal, number of two letters or of all three letters, your representational systems are likely to be equally balanced between these preferences.

Key idea

Most people have a preferred representational system.

Engaging your audience

When people read, their imagination is stimulated and they internally create images, feelings, sounds, tastes and smells. Even though films, plays and television dramas are delivered as images and sounds rather than just words, our imagination still recreates feelings, tastes, smells and also further images and sounds that are not delivered by the camera or sound track. How vividly these are manifested for an individual will depend on how powerful their imagination is and on how strongly they are engaged by the work.

If someone does not engage sufficiently with our work, it is far easier for their attention to stray and for them to give up partway through our story. Even if they persevere until the end, they are unlikely to experience or learn what we hoped they would.

Key idea

When our audience reads or watches our work, their internal representational systems create or recreate the sights, sounds, actions, feelings, tastes and smells. As their representational systems are stimulated, they become engaged with our work.

WRITING THAT ENGAGES ALL THE SENSES

Writers and storytellers guide their audiences to connect to their representational systems by the language they use. In the case of prose writing, this is simply the words they chose. For scriptwriters, their 'language' includes the dialogue, sound effects and images.

When writers use language that connects to all the representational systems, i.e. stimulates all the senses, they:

▶ encourage their audience to use all their senses to engage with their work

▶ ensure that whatever an individual's primary representational system is, it becomes stimulated.

Connecting to all our audience's representational systems will deliver a more engaging experience, so it is usually a good idea to use language that stimulates all the senses whenever possible in your writing.

Case study

The following two pieces of prose contain different amounts of sensory description.

A

Amy sat in the coffee shop wishing Archie was with her.

A woman dropped a mug on the floor behind her. It broke and the pieces skidded beneath Amy's table. But Amy was so lost in thought, she didn't notice. She just sipped her coffee, wishing Archie was there.

B

Amy warmed her hands against the china mug and stared across the empty coffee shop. If only Archie had still been here.

A waitress dropped a mug on the tiled floor behind her. But Amy was so lost in thought, she didn't even hear it smash or notice the shards of china skidding past her shoes. She blew the froth from the top of her coffee and sipped the dark liquid. If only Archie had still been here.

The second piece of prose is more engaging, because it stimulates all the senses and it stimulates them more fully.

Try it now

Identify which representational systems are being stimulated by each sentence in the two pieces of prose you read in the case study. Now check your answers.

Representational systems stimulated in piece A:

1 *Amy sat in the coffee shop wishing Archie was with her.* – visual (Amy, Archie, the coffee shop), olfactory and gustatory (coffee), kinaesthetic (feeling: she's missing him).
2 *A woman dropped a mug on the floor behind her.* – visual.
3 *It broke and the pieces skidded beneath Amy's table.* – visual.
4 *But Amy was so lost in thought, she didn't notice.* – visual (Amy), kinaesthetic (lost in thought).
5 *She just sipped her coffee, wishing Archie was there.* – visual (Amy sipping coffee, Archie), kinaesthetic (action: sipping; feeling: missing Archie) olfactory and gustatory (coffee).

Representational systems stimulated in piece B:

1 *Amy warmed her hands against the china mug and stared across the empty coffee shop.* – visual (coffee shop, Amy, the mug), olfactory and gustatory (coffee), kinaesthetic (feeling: Amy's hands are cold – and if we know Amy's hands are cold, we are likely to assume Amy herself is cold; we also feel both the smoothness and the heat of the mug).

2 *If only Archie had still been here.* – visual (Archie), kinaesthetic (feeling: she's missing him).

3 *A waitress dropped a mug on the tiled floor behind her.* – visual and auditory.

4 *But Amy was so lost in thought; she didn't even hear it smash or notice the shards of china skidding past her shoes.* – visual (Amy, shards of china skidding past her shoes), kinaesthetic (feeling: lost in thought), auditory (the sound of the mug smashing).

5 *She blew the froth from the top of her coffee and sipped the dark liquid.* – visual (blew froth from coffee, Amy sipping coffee, dark liquid), kinaesthetic (action: blowing, sipping), auditory (the sound of her blowing – if you have a highly tuned auditory representational system, you might also have imagined the sound of Amy's breath bursting the bubbles in the froth), olfactory and gustatory (coffee).

6 *If only Archie had still been here.* – visual (Archie), kinaesthetic (feeling: she's still missing Archie).

Key idea

Provoking as many representational systems as strongly as you can ensures that the imagination of every member of your audience is well stimulated. This encourages them to engage with your story as strongly as possible.

When you read the two pieces of prose in the case study, your primary representation system is likely to have produced a stronger reaction to the words that connected to it. The strength of your reaction is also likely to be influenced by the number of times a particular system is stimulated. However, although our primary representational system is not usually our olfactory or gustatory system, when they are stimulated this often produces a highly evocative reaction. This means the word *coffee* may have had the greatest impact on you.

You may also have found that you overlooked the more subtle connections your primary representational system was not engaged by. For example, if your auditory system is not your primary representational system, you may have missed the sounds Amy's breath made.

STIMULATING TWO OR MORE REPRESENTATIONAL SYSTEMS
▶ The olfactory and gustatory systems

You will have noticed that the word *coffee* in the above pieces of prose has the power to recreate both the taste and smell of coffee. This happens because much of what we taste is dictated by what we smell. Therefore, when we read the words such as 'coffee', 'strawberry' and 'pineapple', we are able to recreate both the taste and the smell.

▶ Onomatopoeia

Onomatopoeic words, such as 'scrunch' and 'wobble', create a sound (stimulating the auditory representational system) as well as describing an action (stimulating the kinaesthetic representational system). For example: *The leaves scrunched beneath Emma's feet as she marched up the drive.*

Here we see and hear the leaves being 'scrunched' and experience the action of Emma's foot pushing down on them.

▶ Multitasking verbs

Using a verb that describes not only what is done but also the way something is done – such as the verb 'marched' instead of 'walked' in '*The leaves scrunched beneath Emma's feet as she marched up the drive*' – is another way to convey more information in fewer words.

▶ Visual descriptors

In reality it's almost impossible to describe anything without giving some form of visual description. For example, when we read the word *strawberry*, we see a strawberry in our mind's eye as well as imagining the taste and smell.

ENGAGING ALL REPRESENTATIONAL SYSTEMS WITH YOUR WRITING

When we write we often recreate the places, people, animals and objects we are thinking about in our mind's eye, particularly if our primary representational system is our visual system. Even if the visual system isn't our primary system, it's easy to get lost in what we're describing visually and forget that people, animals, objects and places have sounds, smells, ways of moving, a certain feel and evoke emotional reactions too. Also, in prose writing, even if our primary representational system is kinaesthetic, adding the emotions our characters feel may escape our writing, because we assume our reader is feeling what we feel, so we don't show it.

Try it now

Consider a scene you have written recently.

Prose writers

How often do you stimulate each representational system? How well will this scene engage your audience?

Scriptwriters

How many times is each representational system stimulated by:
* the direction/images?
* the dialogue?
* the soundtrack/sound effects?
How well will this scene engage a script reader?

How well would the final film engage its audience?

Unless your piece feels perfect, rewrite it, pulling in as much sensory detail as possible without making your prose cluttered, or your imagined film cluttered or over-directing those who will work with your script.

Remember this

While it is generally advantageous to produce work that engages all the representational systems more or less equally, a writer may chose to create a particular impact by using specific language to direct their audience to engage with just one or two representational systems, e.g. highlighting smells by using a far higher proportion of words that stimulate the olfactory representational system.

DESCRIPTION, ACTION AND DIALOGUE

When we write we also need to remember:

▶ stimulation of the kinaesthetic representational system is achieved by characters taking action as well as by the way they are feeling

▶ stimulation of the auditory representational system can be achieved by dialogue as well as onomatopoeic words, descriptions of sounds and, in the case of film, sounds themselves.

Achieving a balance between action, description/imagery and dialogue will therefore deepen your audience's sensory experience as well as having an impact on the pacing of your story.

A good way to check the balance you have struck between dialogue, action and description in prose is to work through what you have written using different colour highlighter pens. Highlight each sentence according to whether it is primarily dialogue, action or description. This will give a strong visual representation of the balance, or lack of it, that you have achieved.

Remember this

Great description is about choosing the right images and words rather than writing pages and pages. Although it is important to stimulate different representational systems, it is also important not to let your writing get bogged down by trying to stimulate senses too frequently.

Presupposition: Everyone lives in their own unique model of the world.

Because of different people's varying sensitivities to different sensory input, our representational systems present us with a sensory model of the world unlike anybody else's, i.e. the internal reaction to sensory stimulus is different for everyone. This adds to the uniqueness of the way we sense and interpret the world.

THE IMPACT OF OUR UNIQUE SENSORY PERCEPTIONS
▶ Synaesthesia

The differences in individuals' perceptions and therefore their experience of our writing may be very slight. However, the experience of synaesthesia demonstrates that not everyone's internal representation systems simply recreate smells as smells, visual information as pictures, etc.

Synaesthesia is the term used to describe the intermingling of our senses. People who are considered to be synaesthesic connect senses in an unusual manner. For example, they may see colours when they hear music. However, people who are not considered to be synaesthesic also experience an intermingling of senses. For example, certain pieces of music can influence most people's feelings and affect mood.

▶ Past experience

Past experience influences our sensory responses. For example, Christmas may have been experienced as a child by one person as a magical time and by another as a time of family arguments, and so the images, sounds and feelings associated with their memories of Christmas would be completely different. The mention of childhood Christmases would therefore be likely to evoke very different feelings, images and sounds for each person.

▶ The importance of unique reactions to your writing

It is important to remember your own uniqueness and the uniqueness of your audience when you write. In practice, this means using your understanding to steer a practical path. For example, most people won't imagine colours if your protagonist is listening to Mozart's 'Eine kleine Nachtmusik'. It also probably won't matter if they are synaesthesic and they do imagine colours, because that's the way they always experience music. However, there will be a variety of kinaesthetic reactions in your audience that could matter; ranging from those who love Mozart to those who dislike classical music intensely.

Presupposition: The meaning of a communication is the response you get.

This presupposition reminds us that unless we show a character's reaction, or have previously indicated how they are likely to react, our audience is likely to assume the character has the same reaction as they do. Even if the reaction isn't that important to your story, it will influence the ideas your audience has about that character. This could make the character's reaction seem incongruent with other traits you have given them.

Your characters' representational systems

Because our characters are also 'real people', they too are likely to have a preferred representational system through which they perceive and process the world. Whether or not we are born with an innate preference for one particular representational system, our upbringing can influence us to develop unconscious preferences.

Having an upbringing during which we are encouraged to take part in particular activities can strengthen a specific representational system. For example, if our parents or teachers encourage us to take part in sport, this will strengthen our kinaesthetic system. If they encourage us to play a musical instrument, this will help bring an auditory preference to the fore. If they instil an appreciation of art in us, our visual abilities will grow.

It is important to note here that although being encouraged to engage in particular activities can develop particular representational systems, our unique personal make-up will be developed rather than created by this experience. For example, a child is likely to improve their auditory representational system if they learn to play a musical instrument, but that does not mean they will develop an auditory preference, particularly if they have poor auditory abilities.

The activities we engage in as children therefore develop our perceptual preferences and when one representational system is used more regularly by the activities we engage in, it may become dominant at the cost of the other representational systems. However, most people still regularly use their other representational systems and are reasonably balanced.

Remember this

Taking part in particular activities as we grow up can strengthen a particular representational system.

As we grow up, we tend to choose to engage in activities we excel at and we are often encouraged to pursue careers that involve activities for which we appear to have a natural ability. This means we are usually drawn to hobbies and careers that involve a higher degree of use of our preferred representational system. Taking part in these hobbies and careers will in turn strengthen the representational systems they employ.

Try it now

Consider the perceptual preference(s) that the self-assessment identified you as having. Are these systems reflected in the hobbies you have chosen and/or your job, or perhaps the parts of your job that you are best at?

Think of things you find it difficult to do. Is this also a reflection of your perceptual preference(s)?

YOUR CHARACTERS' HISTORY, OCCUPATIONS AND HOBBIES

Considering the development of people's representational systems highlights once more the importance of having a strong understanding of your characters' life histories and of creating character portraits. (See Chapters 1–3). Their representational systems may have been shaped by engaging strongly in particular interests or activities as children. This in turn may influence the choices they make as adults and how successful they are as adults in the activities they take part in.

The idea that our childhood experiences can shape our perceptual preferences can be used overtly when you create characters. For example, if you want your character to be a world-class cellist who only discovered they could play the cello in their twenties, you can plant seeds in their past that predispose them to having a strong auditory preference.

You may also want to use this idea less overtly. For example, a character's childhood influences on the preferred representational system may lead them to:

▶ be good at certain aspects of their job

▶ be completely hopeless at their job

▶ have certain hobbies.

Try it now

Look again at the character portrait you have created for one of your main characters. Does their personal history tell you why they are good at certain things or why they have pursued a particular hobby or career? What does their past suggested their preferred representational system is?

Remember this

When you are creating characters, the idea of occupations or hobbies being linked to representational preferences can be considered in both directions:

❋ your character's background may suggest they do or are good at doing certain things

❋ their representational preferences and current interests or career may inform you of the type of areas they were likely to be engaged in as a child.

Improving your writing by strengthening your own representational systems

Although we are likely to have a dominant representational system, even as adults we can strengthen our less developed systems. Strengthening all your representational systems can make you more sensually aware when you are researching. It can also make you more aware of engaging all your audience's senses when you write.

We can strengthen our less developed representational systems by:

▶ becoming more aware of the world around us

▶ improving our observational skills

▶ focusing on stimulating all our audience's senses when we write.

Try it now

Use the following exercises to strengthen your representational systems.

❋ Look around a familiar room, taking in all the details. Become really aware of the space and the objects in it. Close your eyes and listen to the sounds around you. Breathe in the smells. Does the room have an atmosphere? Open the window and repeat the exercise.

* Pick up an object. Close your eyes and explore it with your fingers. Now smell it. Even listen to it, if appropriate.
* Listen to a piece of music with your eyes closed. Check in with yourself about how it makes you feel.

Key idea

You can strengthen your own representational systems by deliberately taking in the sights, smells, sounds, tastes and sensations that go on around and within you.

In future, regularly spend time taking in the sights, smells, sounds, tastes and sensations that go on around and within you. Do this with both new and familiar activities and in new and familiar places.

When you write, always re-imagine when you experienced what you are writing about, or imagine a similar experience if you have not engaged in this experience. (See also Chapters 6 and 13.)

Focus points

The main points to remember from this chapter are:

* When our brain uses one of our senses to recreate real or imagined events, it is described by NLP as using a representational system.
* Most people have a preferred representational system, although some people process the world equally through two or more representational systems. However, unless we have a physical inability to perceive a particular sense, we all learn, perceive and recreate the world through all our senses and our feelings.
* When our audience experiences our work, their internal representational systems recreate the sights, sounds, actions, feelings, tastes and smells we offer them. As their representational systems are stimulated, they become engaged with our work.
* Provoking as many representational systems as strongly as you can ensures that the imagination of every member of your audience is

well stimulated. This encourages them to engage with your story as strongly as possible.

✳ You can strengthen your own representational systems by deliberately taking in the sights, smells, sounds, tastes and sensations that go on around and within you.

Next step

This chapter has introduced the idea of representational systems and how what you write influences your audience's imagination. Chapter 8 will build on this understanding by exploring the finer details of how we engage with our senses. It will also explore in greater depth how to create prose that is evocative and engaging.

8

The devil's in the detail

In this chapter you will learn about:

▶ *the concept of submodalities, and how submodalities impact on our writing*

▶ *how Big Chunk–Small Chunk thinking and the level of detail impacts on our writing*

▶ *metaphors and how they impact on our writing*

▶ *a method to 'troubleshoot' the level of detail used.*

Self-assessment: How well are you conveying the finer details?

Choose a scene you have written recently but haven't read for at least two weeks and preferably a month.

Prose writers – read through the scene imagining that you are the intended audience, and answer the questions below.

Scriptwriters – imagine that the script you have written is being developed into a film. Answer the questions below as far as you can, considering the impact you think your directions and dialogue will have on those developing the script. Then answer the questions again, as far as possible, considering the audience watching the final result.

1 How strong are the smells?

2 How bright is the light in the scene?

3 How intensely does the point-of-view character feel their emotions?

4 How loud/rhythmical are the sounds? How near/how far?

5 What language is used to create images in your audience's mind?

6 How strongly do you experience any actions the point-of-view character carries out?

7 How strongly do you experience anything the point-of-view character touches?

Use your answers to help you recognize:

1 If you are a prose writer, how well you have shown the subtleties of the sensory details you are conveying to your audience.

2 If you are a scriptwriter, how well you have shown the subtleties of the sensory details you are conveying to those who will work with your script to bring it to the screen. Remember, however, that you are only drawing to their attention what they need to know but aren't responsible for deciding or can't work out themselves; you shouldn't be trying to teach them their job.

3 If what you want to stand out does stand out.

4 If the scene will leave your audience feeling the way you want it to leave them feeling.

Submodalities

In Chapter 7, we considered the representational systems – visual, auditory, kinaesthetic, olfactory and gustatory – that our brains use to connect to and imagine what we read or see on the screen. However, considering the importance of engaging representational systems is only part of the story. For each representational system, there are also the finer details to consider. ... The sun may be shining, but how bright is it? Music is playing, but how loudly? How hot and how sweet is the coffee? Is our protagonist so angry that they feel as if they will explode or are they simply irritated?

In NLP these finer details are called **submodalities**. Submodalities describe distinctions of form or structure – rather than content – within a sensory representational system.

Try it now

Imagine a scene you are planning to write. Note how dark or bright the light is in your mind's eye, then imagine you are slowly turning up a dimmer-switch that makes the light brighter. Turn the brightness up until the scene is as bright as possible. Now turn it down slowly until the scene is in darkness.

Next, consider the sounds; increase and decrease the volume of each sound element one at a time.

Finally, imagine how your point-of-view character feels. Intensify their emotion until it is twice as strong. How would the scene feel if they didn't care at all?

The exercise above encouraged you to experience and explore some submodalities: brightness within your visual representational system; volume within your auditory representational system, and emotion within your kinaesthetic representational system. However, for each representational system there are many more submodalities to consider.

Typical submodalities

Visual representations (images)	Brightness
	Moving or still
	Fast – slow – still
	Location
	Black and white or colour
	Clear – blurred
	Flat or three-dimensional
	Shape
	Size
	Distance from point of view
	Perspective
Auditory representations (sounds)	Location
	Volume
	Tone
	Pitch
	Tempo
	Soft – harsh
	Distance away
	Rhythm
	Quality
	Continuous – intermittent
	Fading – undulating – increasing
	Number of sound sources
Kinaesthetic representations (emotional and physical sensations, feelings)	Location of a sensation – internal or external
	Strong – weak
	Size
	Texture
	Temperature
	Rhythm
	Pressure
	Still – moving
	Continuous – intermittent
	Fading – changing – increasing
	Intensity
Olfactory and gustatory representations (smell and taste)	Sweetness
	Sourness
	Bitterness
	Savouriness
	Saltiness
	Aversive – appetitive
	Strong – weak

Note that some submodalities offer a continuum of possibilities; for example, volume can exist at many levels. Other submodalities offer one of two options; for example, a sensation is either internal or external.

Key idea

Submodalities describe distinctions of form or structure – rather than content – within a sensory representational system.

Submodalities and your writing

When we write prose, we automatically link to our own sensory representations of what we are imagining, and translate what we imagine onto paper as words. Skilful prose writers translate the intensity of what they are imagining into their writing.

In works written for the screen, the final and more subtle decisions about lighting, sound, location, costumes, etc. are unlikely to be made by the scriptwriter. However, an understanding of submodalities is still important for a scriptwriter, as the dialogue you write will stimulate your audience's representational systems. Furthermore, the finer details of the settings, lighting and sound effects you suggest will enable those working with your script to connect to and understand your vision and translate it in a way you feel happy with.

Case study

The following paragraphs are from the blog *My life under paper*, describing events on the farm of the author, V. Kathryn Evans, on 3 January 2012.

Why I hate the wind

Wind is the weather that frightens me most. I have cowered in a caravan while wind has rocked it like a demented mother. I have stood paralysed while a tornado blackened the sky and ripped its dark path though one greenhouse after another. I have held my breath in the after calm, shocked by the devastation, fearful of its return and grateful that things were not much, much worse.

Yesterday the sky blackened once more.

Visual submodalities

In the first paragraph Evans doesn't tell us the light fades, but skilfully turns the brightness down in our mental picture by describing the

116

tornado as *'blackening the sky'* and *'ripping a dark path'*. She then tweaks the dimmer-switch right down with the line *'Yesterday the sky blackened once more.'*

Kinaesthetic and auditory submodalities
The phrase *'wind has rocked it like a demented mother'* tells of the rhythmic nature and speed of the caravan's movement, and of the wind's strength. This evokes both kinaesthetic and auditory representations within our imaginations. Evans also adds to the rhythm with the description of the tornado ripping its path *'through one greenhouse after another'*.

Our kinaesthetic representational system is also stimulated by Evans' own actions – the word *'paralyse'* describes how still she stood. Holding her breath also adds to the sense of her inability to move. Furthermore, the author's lack of movement contrasts with the description of the strength and ferocity of the wind. This not only builds on our imagining of the wind's strength, but reinforces her fear and vulnerability, which in turn strengthens the emotional response of the reader.

A writer can play with submodalities prior to writing in order to consider whether an image, scene, several scenes or an entire story could be improved in their own imagination before they attempt to write it down.

Try it now

Re-imagine the scene you considered in the self-assessment at the start of this chapter, playing with the submodalities to see if you can improve it. Consider ideas such as:

✳ what would happen if the point-of-view character was closer to the action? Or further away?

✳ what if the weather/lighting made it brighter/darker...?

✳ what if the sounds/voices were louder/quieter...? Harsher/softer...?

✳ what if the smells were stronger?

Rewrite the scene, or a vital image in the scene, paying attention to conveying submodalities without using too much detail or too overtly working on the submodalities.

Remember this

When you're using submodalities to create atmosphere, beware of falling into cliché. For example, ghost stories don't have to take place on pitch-black nights in tumbledown properties.

Big Chunk–Small Chunk thinking

In Chapter 3, we discussed the General vs Specific meta program or Big Chunk vs Small Chunk thinking. Big Chunk–Small Chunk thinking concerns the level of generality or specificity in the way we think; Big Chunk thinking considers the bigger picture, while Small Chunk thinking focuses on details. However, as with other meta programs, there are not just these two extremes of thinking but a continuum, with levels of detail ranging from the big picture right down to the finest detail.

Presupposition: Everyone lives in their own unique model of the world.

As everyone is unique, some people will have a tendency to be overwhelmed by too much detail while others will relish the more minor. So our writing needs to deliver sufficient detail for our audience to understand what we are telling them and to engage strongly with our work, but it must not overwhelm or bore them with too much specificity. Getting the balance right will depend on your audience – which is one of the reasons why it's important to understand the audience you are writing for (see Chapter 11).

As well as ensuring the level of detail is appropriate for our audience, we also need to be constantly aware that there are times when we need to draw the bigger picture, times when our story will benefit from focusing on the minutiae, and times when we need to work somewhere in between. Playing with the Big Chunk–Small Chunk continuum can help us find the right level.

INCREASING AND DECREASING LEVELS OF DETAIL
Chunking down is the term given to increasing the level of detail. **Chunking up** is the term given to decreasing the level of detail.

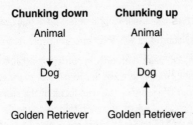

Chunking down	Chunking up
Animal	Animal
↓	↑
Dog	Dog
↓	↑
Golden Retriever	Golden Retriever

As we write, we can deliberately chunk up or chunk down, depending on whether higher or lower levels of detail are appropriate.

Case study

The passage below from V. Kathryn Evans' blog continues her description of the events of 3 January 2012. and demonstrates the use of the general–specific filter within a piece of writing. See how evans focuses on details about the storm and its effects but only briefly outlines other facts and characters. This leads us to engage fully with what she want us to focus on.

I was working on the end of year report when it hit. My computer switched off. The power was out. In a heartbeat the gusting wind outside changed to a tearing, rain lashed storm force 10. Fence panels and gas canisters blew past my office window. My first thought was for the children.

Safe at school. Solid, brick built, sturdy school.

But where was Beloved? I threw my coat on and battled outside. The rain was tidal, lashing in horizontal waves, the wind threatened to tip me over.

Evans starts with three short Big-Chunk sentences: *'I was working on the end of year report when it hit. My computer switched off. The power was out.'* They carry little detail, because their purpose is just to place the point-of-view character. In contrast, the next two sentences, where the action really begins are laced with Small-Chunk detail: *'the gusting wind outside changed to a tearing, rain lashed storm force 10. Fence panels and gas canisters blew past my office window.'*

Although Evan's first thought is her children, they are irrelevant to the story. She therefore dismisses them with two abrupt sentences that confirm their safety: *'Safe at school. Solid, brick built, sturdy school.'*

Notice here also that the Small-Chunk detail 'brick built' creates a strong immediate understanding in the reader.

Evans' husband is also dealt with only in sufficient detail to explain her fear and relationship: *'But where was Beloved?'* She then returns to Small-Chunk details about the storm – the true focus of the story: *'The rain was tidal, lashing in horizontal waves, the wind threatened to tip me over.''*

HOW WELL DO YOU DRAW DETAIL IN YOUR STORIES?

As a unique human being, you may:

▶ have a tendency to paint your stories with broad brush strokes, or

▶ in vivid detail, or

▶ focus on some point on the continuum between Big Chunk and Small Chunk thinking, or

▶ move between Big Chunk and Small Chunk thinking, putting in the amount of detail you believe is appropriate.

Try it now

Look back at a scene from your current work in progress and consider, for both description and dialogue:

✻ where do you focus on detail?

✻ does the detail you place work well?

✻ do you put in too much detail?

✻ are there places where there is too little detail?

✻ do you appear to have a tendency towards consistently Big Chunk or Small Chunk writing?

✻ are there parts that would benefit from chunking up or chunking down further?

✻ are there points where you avoid chunking down to save work?

Our thinking styles are habitual, rather than hardwired. Therefore, if the exercise led you to realize that you don't habitually move between Big Chunk and Small Chunk writing when necessary, this awareness should help you to recognize where different levels of detail are needed in your work.

Be aware also of the impact of different levels in your work and seek to improve your skill in this area if you feel it is necessary.

Remember this

For scriptwriters the details are contained both in their characters' dialogue and in the directions they give to those who will work on their script. The level of detail scriptwriters give in dialogue and directions is just as important as the level of detail that prose writers put into their work.

Key idea

When we write, we need to chunk up or chunk down along the continuum of detail to find exactly the right level of specificity.

FILLING IN THE BLANKS

When good writers translate the intensity of what they are imagining into their writing, they do it in a subtle manner without overloading an image or scene by adding each and every detail associated with it. Instead the writer trusts their audience to use their own experiences and imagination to flesh out the details they are given. This is demonstrated by the extracts quoted in the two case studies in this chapter:

1   In the extract in the first case study, the increasing darkness and the image of the storm influence our kinaesthetic representational system to lower the temperature in our imagination without temperature even being mentioned.

2   In the extracts in both case studies, there is only one detail about Evans' experience out in the storm – the wind threatens to tip her over. However, in our imaginations as we read the final paragraph we see a woman battling to stay upright, her hair blowing over her face, her clothes billowing and gusting around her. By focusing on her fear (in the first extract) and the details of the wind and its impact (in both extracts), Evans has a painted a vivid picture of the storm and our imagination has filled in the remainder.

DETAILS AND TIME

Our audience's imagination doesn't just build a sensory reconstruction when we impart detail. Level of detail and how it is presented can also impact on our audience's sense of time.

Generally, the more detail that is given, the more slowly time seems to pass. You may have noticed that in the piece used in the case studies above, Evans holds us back from the story of what happen on 3 January 2012 with details of her past experience. This has the effect of slowing down the time before the storm strikes and builds our anticipation of impending disaster. Adding a greater amount of detail also increases the time it takes a reader to read and imagine it or see it unfold, or, in the case of dialogue, it takes longer for an actor to say the words.

Remember this

There are no 'right answers' to how much or what detail to give in a piece of writing. What you use will depend on many things, including:

* the purpose of a scene
* the type of scene
* the type of story
* your audience
* the effects you want to create
* what you want to draw attention to
* what you want to hide
* your personal style.

Metaphors

A **metaphor** is an image, story or tangible entity used to describe or represent something in a way that is abstract or not literally applicable. For example, a character who was being ignored might say, '*I was a mouse with the tiniest of squeaks.*'

Metaphors are useful to writers for many reasons:

▶ Metaphors paint pictures, stories or scenes with a minimal use of words – for example describing the feelings associated with being '*a mouse with the tiniest of squeaks*' would take a lot more than the nine words used in the metaphor.

▶ Metaphors are expressed in symbolic language – symbolic language is able to 'slip past' the conscious mind and connect to the audience's emotional subconscious, engaging them at an emotional level. Using the phrase *'I sank without casting a ripple in the pond'* allows the audience to connect to their own personal reactions and feelings about what is happening to the viewpoint character and therefore engages the audience more effectively than if they say, *'I was alone'* or *'I was friendless'* or *'Nobody noticed me'*.

▶ Metaphors encourage your audience to open their imagination – if a character or narrator says something such as, *'I was angry'* or *'I was upset'* or *'I was frustrated'*, they offer the audience a label for a feeling and give them nothing further to think about. If they say *'I was about to boil over'*, they encourage the audience to create an image and make their own interpretation of the character's feelings.

▶ Metaphors add life to language – replacing familiar words and phrases with fresh new metaphors adds interest and life to what we offer our audience. For example, saying *'she was the eye that saw everything'* feels fresher and engages the reader more strongly than *'she was our neighbourhood busybody'*.

Remember this

Some metaphors make for bad writing. These include:

✳ common metaphors that have become clichés, e.g. *'our love was a battlefield'*
✳ awkward or silly metaphors – unless you're writing comedy, e.g. *'I was a pigeon sitting on the window ledge of life and she was the householder tired of my droppings soiling her patio.'*
✳ using too many metaphors.

METAPHORS AND DIALOGUE

Some characters will use metaphors in their dialogue and some won't. The metaphors they choose will depend on the character themselves and may well reflect their background, personality, age and education. Metaphors used by your characters might also be linked to their jobs, pastimes and personal preoccupations. Depending on who your character is, it might also be fine for them to use clichéd metaphors – people do in real life. It might also be acceptable for a character to use awkward or silly metaphors or to overuse them. However, whatever metaphors you do choose to use, take care that what you choose is appropriate.

Try it now

Look back at a short piece of writing you have created recently. If it is devoid of metaphors or might benefit from a few more, have a go at developing one or two for:

✻ some of the explanations or descriptions you have written
✻ within the dialogue.

If your work already contains plenty of metaphors, consider:

✻ is it overloaded with metaphors?
✻ are all the metaphors working well?

USING METAPHORS WITH GREATER DIVERSITY

A metaphor doesn't just have to be expressed in the form of a person or object being something else. They can be used in various other ways, including as:

▶ verbs: 'The news about Ali *salvaged* her dignity.'

▶ adjectives and adverbs: 'His *ravenous* lust swallowed her whole.'

▶ prepositional phrases: 'She charmed me with *the tongue of a viper.*'

Key idea

Metaphors are useful to the writer because they can:

✻ vastly reduce the amount of description required
✻ connect powerfully with your audience's emotional subconscious
✻ open up your audience's imagination
✻ engage your audience more strongly
✻ add life to the language you use.

Troubleshooting detail

Sometimes you may feel a piece of writing isn't working or you receive feedback that it is cluttered with detail, too sparse in detail or people are missing what you wanted it to convey. If that happens, the following questions may help you to identify what to focus on and/or where not to put so much emphasis.

▶ Who/what is important in this scene/image?

▶ Whose story is this? Just because it is someone's story, it doesn't mean that the majority of the description has to be about them. For example, the story used in the earlier case studies belongs to V. Kathryn Evans, but she makes very little reference to herself; the majority of the description is about the storm.

▶ What is important to my point-of-view character? Is the same thing important to the story? If not, what is important to the story?

▶ What is the point of the piece?

▶ Where is the heart of my story/scene?

▶ Where is the real action?

▶ Am I trying to put too much information into too short a space?

▶ Am I trying to rush the action and putting in too little detail?

▶ Is there too much dialogue and not enough description?

▶ What does my audience really need to know at this point?

▶ What does my audience need to feel right now?

▶ Who/what do I need to focus on right now?

▶ What is just 'scenery' and what is important?

▶ Does my story/this scene start too slowly?

▶ Does my story/this scene start too quickly?

▶ Does my audience need to pause here, becoming engulfed in the moment or simply be informed about something?

▶ Do I need to slow this scene down or speed it up?

▶ Am I only keeping this in because I really like the way I've written it?

▶ Would the whole of this idea be better summarized as a metaphor?

Remember this

Good manipulation of detail alone does not create good writing – it is just one tool in a writer's toolkit.

Focus points

The main points to remember from this chapter are:

❋ Submodalities describe distinctions of form or structure – rather than content – within a sensory representational system.

❋ When we write, we need to chunk up or chunk down on the continuum of detail to find the right level of specificity.

❋ A metaphor is an image, story or tangible entity used to describe or represent something in a way that is abstract or not literally applicable.

❋ The use of submodalities, details and metaphors creates texture and flow within a piece of writing, stimulating our audience's representational systems in an ever-changing variety of ways, engaging them in our writing, opening their imaginations and focusing their attention more strongly on some ideas than on others.

❋ There are no 'right answers' to how much or what detail to give in a piece of writing.

Next step

In Part 2, we have mostly considered how writers, communicate with their audiences. Chapter 9 will consider the subtleties that exist in our characters' communication, both with one another and with our audience, beyond just the words they use.

Part 3

Communication, connection and conflict

9

Unspoken messages

In this chapter you will learn about:

- ▶ *non-verbal signals used in communication*
- ▶ *ways that non-verbal signals can be used to improve your writing and your characters.*

Self-assessment for prose writers: How well do you convey unspoken messages?

Read though a scene of your work in progress. Using a different colour pen for each character, highlight each time you convey, however subtly, a **non-viewpoint** character's:

1 posture (beyond just saying whether they are standing or sitting)

2 facial expressions

3 gestures

4 movements/actions

5 breathing

6 tone of voice, volume, pitch, tempo, rhythm or quality

7 changes in skin tone.

Highlight also any messages given to your audience or other characters through any non-viewpoint character's appearance or proximity to others.

What you have highlighted tells your audience about what your non-viewpoint characters think or feel. Apart from the words they say, these messages are the only way your audience knows what the characters are thinking or feeling.

Use what you have highlighted to identify whether you have conveyed everything you want to tell your audience about what each non-viewpoint character is thinking or feeling but not expressing in words.

Self-assessment for scriptwriters: How well do you convey unspoken messages?

Read though a scene of your work in progress. Using a different colour pen for each character, highlight each time you convey, however subtly, a character's:

1 posture (beyond just saying whether they are standing or sitting)

2 facial expressions

3 gestures

4 movements/actions

5 breathing

6 tone of voice, volume, pitch, tempo, rhythm or quality

7 changes in skin tone.

Highlight also any messages given to your audience or other characters through any non-viewpoint character's appearance or proximity to others.

What you have highlighted tells your audience something about what your characters think or feel. Actors will generally convey 'non-verbal communication' as they see fit through their acting. Directors will also have a say in determining non-verbal signals, while wardrobe and make-up will also contribute to developing a character's appearance. However, despite others determining much of the non-verbal communication, there are times when non-verbal signals can make a huge difference to what the audience perceives and these need to be made known to anyone reading your script. Look back at what you have highlighted and consider:

1 Is everything I have highlighted necessary or am I trying to teach actors/directors/wardrobe how to do their job?

2 Are there places where those reading my script need more information about what is being communicated non-verbally?

Beyond the words we use

It is not just the words we use that tell people what we are thinking. The **non-verbal signals** we use also send information to other people about what we're thinking and feeling. The same is true for our characters, who send non-verbal signals both to our audience and to the other characters about what they are thinking.

Non-verbal signals are a useful tool for writers, because they can:

▶ reveal the unspoken thoughts and ideas of both viewpoint and non-viewpoint characters

▶ put across a point more subtly or more succinctly than if a character explained what they thought or felt

▶ put across a point more profoundly than if a character explained what they thought or felt

> reveal inconsistency between what a character says and what they think or feel.

Case study

These two pieces of writing demonstrate how the introduction of non-verbal signals can give an audience more information than dialogue alone and deliver a different message to that of the dialogue.

A

'Do you know who broke my vase?' asked Mum.

'Yes,' said Tommy. 'It was Marmalade. She jumped in through the window and knocked it over.'

B

'Do you know who broke my vase?' asked Mum.

'Yes.' Tommy looked down at his feet. 'It was Marmalade,' he answered quietly. 'She jumped in through the window and knocked it over.'

The first piece gives us no reason to doubt Tommy's word. In the second piece, however, Tommy's body language and the quietening of his voice suggest that Marmalade is being framed for a crime she didn't commit or at least that Tommy knows something he isn't saying.

Note also that when non-verbal signals are presented to you, you tend believe them rather than believing what a character says. In other words, not only can we all read non-verbal signals, we put more trust in them than in people's words.

Key idea

Our characters send *non-verbal signals* to one another and to our audience.

Reading non-verbal signals

Although some people are much better than others at picking up on non-verbal signals, we all naturally read them – it just usually happens beyond our conscious awareness. However, we can become better at noticing the non-verbal messages people use.

Here are some of the things you may find it useful to observe in other people in order to become more familiar with non-verbal signals.

▶ Posture

Whether we are standing, sitting or lying down, our posture can give away the mood we're in … happy, relaxed, sad, fearful, pensive, argumentative, paying full attention, bored, tired, confused, etc.

▶ Gestures and body movements

We all make unconscious movements and gestures. For example, some people tilt their head at an angle when they are listening.

▶ Breathing

We can breathe into our upper, middle or lower chest. Breathing can be short and quick, laboured and heavy or deep and slow, depending on who we are and how we feel. Sighing is also another way we express ourselves through our breathing.

▶ Voice

Voices can vary in tone, volume, pitch, tempo, rhythm and quality. People also sometimes make noises that give away thoughts or mood, e.g. clearing their throat, perhaps because they are nervous, or humming, perhaps because they are happy.

▶ Skin tone

The colour of a individual's skin can vary enormously. An extreme example of this is blushing when we are embarrassed. However, there can be more subtle changes linked to our emotional state, which can only be interpreted if we know what an individual's skin tone is like when they are relaxed.

▶ Facial expressions

The movement of our eyes, mouths and facial muscles can all combine to create a huge variety of facial movements. Some are more subtle than others, some may be only fleeting, and others may be held for some time.

▶ Proximity

The distance between people in a social situation often demonstrates the relationship between them. However, it may also be dependent on the social setting, and ranges are different in different cultures. Edward T. Hall who introduced proxemics (the study of measurable distance between people as they interact with one another) identified the following:

▶ Intimate distance – our intimate space is approximately the 18 inches (46 cm) that surrounds us. We are usually only comfortable allowing lovers, children, family members, close friends and pets to breach it.

▶ Personal distance – our personal space extends from around 18 inches (46 cm) to about 4 feet (122 cm) away from us. This space is used in conversations with friends, to chat with associates and in group discussions.

▶ Social distance – our social space ranges from 4–8 feet (1.2–2.4 m) away from us. This is the closest we are comfortable having strangers, newly formed groups and new acquaintances.

These approximate distances are the ones people feel comfortable with in the western world. Breaching them tends to create discomfort and may be done intentionally, e.g. to intimidate. Breaches can also be unintentional, e.g. on a crowded train or busy street. However, people who live in crowded places or habitually use busy modes of public transport tend to become more comfortable with breaches of these distances.

▶ **Appearance**

The choices we make over the way we present ourselves to the world also sends non-verbal messages to those around us. The clothes we wear, the way we style our hair, whether we wear make-up, etc. all send out a statement about our ways of thinking and about how we are feeling.

Try it now

For the next few days and without intruding into their personal business, observe the variety in people's non-verbal signals without assigning any meaning to them. When you have done this for a few days, observe and decide what their non-verbal signals are telling you.

Key idea

We can learn to become better at reading and understanding the non-verbal signals people use.

NLP and non-verbal signals

Many schools of thought take a 'one-size-fits-all' approach to non-verbal signals, ascribing the same meanings to certain postures, gestures or movements regardless of whose body language is being considered. Indeed, the case study above assumed that readers would interpret Tommy's non-verbal signals as an indication that he was lying or covering something up.

Presuppositions:

▶ *Everyone lives in their own unique model of the world.*

▶ *The meaning of a communication is the response you get.*

NLP agrees that there are similarities between people's non-verbal signals and that some responses, such as smiling when we are happy, are largely universal. However, it considers that we all have our own individual patterns.

In other words, Tommy's failure to make eye contact with his mother and lowering his voice as he spoke may not have meant that he was lying or covering something up. Maybe he was just uncomfortable at being put on the spot, maybe he was worried Mum would be cross with Marmalade, or maybe something else.

NLP's idea that we all have a unique system of non-verbal signals can be useful in helping the writer create unique characteristics in their characters. However, it's important also to remember that our audience may take a different meaning from a character's non-verbal signals than the one we intended, because they are consciously or subconsciously applying a generalization, or their own interpretation, of what the non-verbal language means. The presupposition *'The meaning of a communication is the response you get'* reminds us to be wary of this and that what we write may not be interpreted in the way we expect.

Using non-verbal signals in your writing

Using non-verbal signals in your writing is a useful way to inform your audience about what your characters are thinking. With a single movement or vocal description you can show them something that it might take many words of explanation or dialogue to reveal. You can also reveal the unspoken thoughts of non-point-of-view characters that it might otherwise be impossible to reveal without using unrealistic or clumsy dialogue. Furthermore, non-verbal signals not only economize on the words used, but 'show' rather than 'tell' the audience what is happening inside your characters' heads.

Case study

In the following excerpt, taken from Jon Mayhew's novel *Mortlock*, the protagonist, Josie Chrimes, performs a knife-throwing act. In this scene Mayhew shows us what everyone is thinking and feeling even though the only thought he reveals is that the audience is *'eager to spot a trickle of blood'*.

She reached her arm back, then snapped forward and, with a confident flick of her wrist, sent the knife whirling towards its target.

The sound of the audience's gasp made her smile. The knife flashed across the stage until – with a thunk! – it pinned the Great Cardamom's top hat to the corkboard behind him. Knife after knife had described his outline, so close that Josie had seen the front rows of the audience craning forward, wide-eyed, eager to spot a trickle of blood. But now this last knife had hit its mark, Cardamom stepped neatly from under his hat, still pinned to the cork, and smoothed his red hair. With a flourish, he gave a deep bow, looking over at Josie to share a secret wink. The crowd went wild, clapping and cheering.

Key idea

A single movement, vocal change or aspect of someone's appearance can tell our audience something that it might otherwise take a large amount of explanation or dialogue to reveal.

Developing your characters' non-verbal signals

There is no substitute in fiction for well-developed characters. Along with identifying the more static qualities of our characters' visual appearance, such as height, body shape, hair colour, etc., we also need to develop an impression of their characteristic postures, gestures, vocal inflexions, etc. Even if we are writing a script and know our characters will be interpreted and developed further by actors and directors, we still need to have a strong all-round understanding of our characters to write them convincingly. And at times, we may wish to introduce certain non-verbal signals into the script.

Remember this

Developing unique non-verbal signals in our characters can add to their individuality.

As with most aspects of developing our characters, this is a chicken and egg situation. We can assign certain non-verbal signals to a character or we can develop other aspects of them and 'watch' their non-verbal signals emerge.

Try it now

Identify a scene in your work in progress where your main character tells a lie, feels uncomfortable, experiences conflict or tries to hide emotion. Imagine you are another character in the scene. Play through the scene in your mind (more than once if necessary), taking note of your main character's postures, gestures, facial expressions, skin tone, breathing and vocal inflexions.

Remember this

Building a character can take time. Sometimes we need to keep revisiting a question about them because we can't find an answer or find only partial answers. Returning again and again in the creation process is fine. What matters ultimately is that everything a character does is congruent with who they are, what they think and how they feel.

Like any writing device, non-verbal signals can be used badly as well as to good effect. The following are therefore worth considering.

- How familiar your audience is with your characters

- Avoiding cliché

- The variety of non-verbal signals you use

- Developing unique non-verbal signals

- Repetition of non-verbal signals.

CONSIDERING HOW FAMILIAR YOUR AUDIENCE IS WITH YOUR CHARACTERS

The more your audience meets a character, the more they will learn about them. When people read a story, after a while they will subconsciously, and possibly consciously, apply what they already know about a character's beliefs, values, emotional state, etc. and draw conclusions of their own about the character's internal reactions with little or no prompting. However, at the outset of a story, when our audience is learning about a character, they may need more clues. Whatever stage of familiarity with a character your audience has reached, it is important to maintain appropriate non-verbal responses, and not to 'overdo' them so that they become intrusive or even laughable. Good writing usually should pass on non-verbal signals in a discreet way, rather than bludgeoning the audience with them. Exceptions to this do apply, for example in some types of comedy.

Remember this

One of the keys to using non-verbal signals well is to build your character up realistically in the eyes of your audience.

AVOIDING CLICHÉ

There are common non-verbal signals that large numbers of people use to display particular feelings, thoughts, etc. It may be appropriate to use some of these in your writing. However, too many or too obvious a use of the 'usual' responses can make a piece of writing feel clichéd. Don't settle for the first idea or description you think of. Also, consider how your character may be responding with a degree of individuality and/or how you can phrase a well-known response in a fresh new way.

Try it now

Prose writers

Take a book that you consider well written. Read a few pages, noting how the author phrases their characters' non-verbal responses to keep them fresh and interesting.

Scriptwriters

Read through the script of a film you consider well written. Note what sort of instructions the scriptwriter gives to explain the non-verbal responses they require from the actors.

Remember this

Originality needs to blend in and be suitable for the audience you're writing for. Better to write a 'usual' response than make your audience uncomfortable with a description that is clumsy, confusing or makes a character behave in a way that jars because it is so out of the ordinary.

USING A VARIETY OF NON-VERBAL SIGNALS

Don't just stick to one type of signal. Remember that non-verbal signals include posture, facial expressions, gestures, movement, breathing, vocal tone, volume, pitch, tempo, rhythm or quality, changes in skin tone, proximity and appearance.

Try it now

Look back at what you highlighted in the self-assessment at the start of this chapter. Do you rely heavily on showing unspoken thoughts and feelings with a particular type of non-verbal signal? If you do, what different non-verbal signals could you use to show these thoughts and feelings?

DEVELOPING UNIQUE NON-VERBAL SIGNALS

NLP's idea that there is no one-size-fits-all set of non-verbal signals encourages us to explore not just moving away from cliché, but also to developing unique responses in our characters. It can be argued that no behavioural response is truly unique to an individual. However, responses can be developed that seem unique by:

▶ being unusual

▶ adding objects or motifs, e.g. a character clenching their fist when trying to hang on to their self-control is not necessarily a unique action, but if we put a tattoo on their knuckles, the gesture becomes more personal

▶ focusing repeatedly on an individual's particular response so it becomes a character quirk

▶ exaggerating a common response

▶ having only that character respond in that way within the group of characters in a story. For example, in a horror story, one person who always moves to the back of the group each time something makes the group fearful.

REPETITION OF NON-VERBAL SIGNALS

Repeating non-verbal signals can be very powerful. If a character uses a particular non-verbal signal each time they think the same thing, after a while the audience only needs to see or hear the signal to know exactly what the character is thinking. We probably all remember teachers who, with one look, could silence a class, tell a pupil to go to the headmaster's office or inform someone they had just been given a detention.

Remember this

Most people usually read non-verbal signals on an unconscious level, so our audience will not necessarily be aware that they are reading non-verbal signals unless these are particularly overt or repeated. Even then, the audience may still not realize that is what it is doing.

Increasing the strength of a repeated signal can also show that a character's feelings are becoming stronger. For example, increasing the rate at which a character drums their fingers on the table could denote them losing patience or becoming more and more anxious.

While repetition can be a powerful tool in describing behavioural responses and defining characters, it's important not to use it too often. Over-repetition of any device will stand out and make your audience either laugh or become irritated that you're trying too hard. Who your audience is will affect what constitutes too much repetition, and if you're trying to make your audience laugh, then repetition that makes them laugh is what you're looking for. However, a joke can wear thin with too much repetition, and you want be sure – as when you craft any humour – that your audience is laughing at the joke and not at the way you have written it.

STRIKING THE BALANCE BETWEEN VERBAL AND NON-VERBAL COMMUNICATION

Varying statistics can be found about the percentages of verbal and non-verbal communication people use. However, the exact percentages are irrelevant when it comes to considering our writing. This is because prose writers divulge only a certain amount of what is happening in any given scene and leave their readers to fill in the gaps (see Chapters 6 and 8) and in films and TV dramas, actors usually add their own non-verbal communications to a script. Furthermore, although many statistics report that verbal communication is only a small percentage of our total communication, writers, especially scriptwriters, usually give far more lines of dialogue to their characters than they give lines of description of non-verbal signals. Personal style and what feels right for each character and the piece itself are therefore far more important than how much people use verbal and non-verbal communication in real life.

Focus points

The main points to remember from this chapter are:

✳ Our posture, gestures, facial expressions, voices, skin tone, breathing, proximity and appearance can all send non-verbal signals to others about what we are thinking.

✳ We can learn to become better at reading and understanding the non-verbal signals people use.

✳ NLP sees everyone as being unique. It agrees that there are similarities between our non-verbal signals, but considers that we all have our own individual patterns of signals.

✳ A single non-verbal signal can convey unspoken thoughts and feelings to our audience in a concise and effective manner.

✳ Just like any writing device, non-verbal signals can be used badly as well as to good effect.

Next step

Now we have explored the non-verbal signals our characters use to communicate, Chapter 10 will consider character compatibility and how verbal and non-verbal signals can demonstrate both connection and conflict between characters.

10

Connection and conflict between characters

In this chapter you will learn about:

▶ *the concept of rapport, and how people develop rapport with one another*

▶ *how the level of rapport between your characters demonstrates how they are thinking and the strength of their relationships*

▶ *ways to demonstrate the level of rapport between your characters.*

? Self-assessment: How well do your characters relate to one another?

1 Write a list pairing your main character (or one of your main characters) with each of the other major characters in your work in progress.

2 Score on a scale of 1–10 how well each pairing gets on with one another for the majority of your story, where 1 = have a very bad relationship and 10 = have an excellent relationship. If any pairing veers regularly between getting on well and not getting on well, or their compatibility changes dramatically between the start and finish of the story, give them two scores; one for when they get on well and one for when they don't.

For example, if your main character is called Percy and your other major characters are Annabel, Sita, Olaf and Gregory, your list might look like this:

Percy and Annabel	3
Percy and Sita	10
Percy and Olaf	2/9
Percy and Gregory	6

Starting with the first pairing on your list, read through a scene where each pairing interacts with each other.

1 How do you demonstrate to your audience the scores you have given on the list?

2 Do you demonstrate to your audience the scores you have given on your list?

3 If a score is not demonstrated, how does your audience know how well the couple get on with each other?

Rapport

Being in **rapport** with someone is often described as being 'on the same wavelength' or 'in tune' with them. We may be deep in conversation or saying nothing, but whatever we are doing, there is harmony between us and trust and cooperation develop. When people lack rapport, there is disharmony between them and trust and cooperation fail to develop. Rapport is therefore essential to effective communication and vital in building and maintaining successful relationships.

Building rapport with others is a natural skill and most of the time we achieve rapport without even thinking about it. Some people are better at building rapport than others, but for almost all of us there are people we have rapport with and others we find it less easy to communicate with. Most of us have had the experience of meeting someone that we instantly 'connected' with – maybe even feeling as if we'd 'known them all our life'. Most of us have also had the experience of knowing someone but never quite feeling comfortable talking to them.

Although we usually have a general level of rapport with certain people, levels of rapport fluctuate in any relationship. This can vary from a slight rise or fall in the strength of our rapport, e.g. if somebody is a little tired and not quite as communicative as usual, to dramatic changes, e.g. if people have an argument. Therefore, although we tend to have a general level of rapport with others, that level is not static.

Key idea

Rapport is the degree of harmony, trust, connection and cooperation that exists within a relationship. The level of rapport between any two individuals can fluctuate. These fluctuations can be minor or extreme.

Although rapport is a natural phenomenon and rapport-building a natural skill, NLP considers that individuals can enhance and develop this skill. If we study the aspects NLP considers when teaching people to develop their rapport skills, we can explore how to:

▶ demonstrate rapport between our characters more effectively (see the rest of this chapter)

▶ build rapport with our audience more successfully (see Chapter 11).

How do people create rapport?

There are three main influences on the rapport people build:

▶ the common ground they share

▶ the communication skills of those involved

▶ circumstances.

COMMON GROUND

Because rapport is about being 'on the same wavelength' as someone else, the more people have in common with each other, the more easily they are likely to achieve strong rapport. Stronger rapport is more likely to exist or be built when people:

▶ share the same or similar beliefs

▶ share the same or similar values

▶ have shared memories or a common past

▶ are operating compatible thinking filters

▶ are in the same or similar emotional state (although there are exceptions to this).

Try it now

Identify someone you find it easy to talk to. Consider what you know of their beliefs, values and past experiences. What do you have in common in each area? Next, identify someone you find it hard to talk to. Consider what you know of their beliefs, values and past experiences. Identify what you have in common in each area.

You should find that you are aware of having more in common with the person you find it easy to talk to.

Presupposition: Everyone lives in their own unique model of the world.

The idea that we all perceive and recreate the world in our own unique way comes into play when we consider the common ground people share. Because we all use the processes of deletion, distortion and generalization to comprehend the world around us and to create memories, one person may not have the same memories of the same experience as another (see Chapter 6). The experience may also not have impacted on their beliefs and values in the same way. Therefore, just because two people have encountered the same or apparently similar life experiences, it doesn't mean they will see eye to eye over those experiences. People may therefore still struggle to create good rapport even when memories, beliefs, etc. created from common ground are discussed.

Remember this

In general, the more we recognize – consciously or subconsciously – that we have in common with someone, the stronger our rapport with them is likely to be.

COMMUNICATION SKILLS

The degree of rapport between people is also influenced by their individual communication skills. Some people are naturally good at communicating and therefore building rapport, while others have poor communication skills and tend to struggle generally or fail to build rapport. However, even people who have strong communication skills can find it difficult to build strong rapport with poor communicators or those they find it difficult to connect with.

Effective communication consists of two parts: speaking and listening. No conversation can take place unless the parties to it both speak and listen. (Even two lovers sitting silently together are simultaneously listening and speaking – non-verbally- to each other.)

The five main skills we employ when we communicate well are:

▶ immediacy – keeping up with the conversation and paying full attention to both the verbal and non-verbal responses

▶ genuineness – taking genuine interest in the conversation

▶ empathy – when listening, this means being able to imagine yourself in the speaker's place and understand their perspective. It does not necessarily mean that you feel how they feel, but that you understand what they feel

▶ respect – respecting the other person/people taking part in the conversation and allowing them to express and explain their views and beliefs

▶ seeking clarification – seeking clarification when you don't understand what the person who is speaking is saying.

Remember this

In general, the stronger our communication skills, the stronger our rapport with others is likely to be.

CIRCUMSTANCES

The strength of the rapport we create in any relationship at any given time will also depend on the situation we are in.

Sometimes we can have a lot in common with someone, but disagree over one idea that is very important to us and therefore fail to build rapport if that is the subject under discussion. Equally, we only need to share one commonality to build strong rapport if that is what is on the agenda. For example, if we believe in a cause such as saving white tigers from extinction, we could have strong rapport while campaigning for our cause, but have very little else in common with those we are campaigning with.

The circumstances we find ourselves in influence not just the beliefs, values and memories that we expose to others, but also the thinking patterns we operate and our state. These will in turn impact on the rapport we build.

Remember this

The strength of rapport can increase, decrease or be maintained during a single interaction depending on what happens within that interaction.

Conflict and connection between your characters

In the self-assessment at the start of this chapter you were asked to consider your main character's key relationships and the general level of rapport that existed within them. If you have created realistic characters, your main character should have different scores for at least some of their relationships. However, as explained above, the rapport score for any two people can vary. Changes in rapport can be brief, e.g. a miscommunication that leads to you buying a friend the wrong drink in a bar, or more enduring, e.g. the loss of trust when a spouse has an affair.

Although writers rarely need to spend much time considering the level of rapport between their characters, they should ensure that the strength of the rapport that exists at any given moment is congruent with who the characters are, how they are feeling and the situation they find themselves in. For example, it's no good making someone who generally lacks empathy suddenly exhibit concern about other people without a good reason for that change.

If you have created a strong character portrait for your major characters, you should be aware of what common ground they have, how well they communicate and how they are likely to react to the situation they are in. However, you are not at the mercy of your characters when it comes to the strength of rapport they have with one another. You have the power to build, change or destroy the rapport that exists between them. You just need to find the right way to do it. (See Chapter 4.)

Case study

In the 2007 film *The Bucket List*, Edward Cole treats everyone he meets with rudeness and contempt, making him a difficult man to develop rapport with. When he is diagnosed with lung cancer, Edward is forced to share a hospital room with Carter Chambers, a man who appears to be his complete opposite:

✻ Carter is genial, modest and polite; Edward is unfriendly, brash and rude

✻ Carter is married to the only woman he has ever had sex with; Edward has been married four times and is generally promiscuous

* Carter is a family man; Edward is a playboy
* Carter is a car mechanic; Edward is a health tycoon
* Carter has faith; Edward has none.

While they apparently lack common ground and Edward generally lacks good communication skills, good rapport builds between them because of the following main influences:

Circumstances/Common ground:
* They have the same illness.
* They share the experience of the physical torment and indignities of chemotherapy.
* They are both given a terminal diagnosis but want to get more out of life before they die.

Common ground:
* They are both men who have made their own way in the world and lack any sense that one is better than the other.

Communication:
* They deal with their situation with a sense of humour that they both understand.
* They deal with each other's ups and downs not with pity, but with true understanding.

Therefore, although on the surface the two men appear a poor match and initially fail to bond, when circumstances are right, they find common ground, communicate strongly and have strong rapport much of the time.

Try it now

Consider the relationship between two of your main characters and their general level of rapport. Compare their beliefs and values.
* What do they share that creates strong rapport or could build strong rapport between them?
* What creates or could create conflict or lack of rapport between them?

THE RELATIONSHIPS BETWEEN YOUR CHARACTERS

At the start of a story, some characters will already know one another and the general strength of their rapport will have already been established. This simply needs communicating to the audience and then adjusting depending on the situations the characters find themselves in.

Characters who meet during a story will start from nothing. There are no rules to how quickly or how well rapport should build, or whether it should be created at all. Rapport can build slowly or there can be a gradual recognition – both for the characters and/or the audience – that two characters are/aren't on the same wavelength. Rapport can also bloom in an instant when two people immediately feel a connection to each other, even if they can't consciously recognize what creates the instantaneous connection. Equally, people can instantly feel negative about someone when they have merely walked into the room.

As the creator of your characters, you should be able to recognize the underlying reasons for the speed that rapport builds or fails to build. However, remember that just because rapport builds or fails to build instantly, it doesn't mean that the level of rapport has to remain the same throughout a relationship. Remember also that the degree of rapport achieved at any given point should feel right and natural for the circumstances and the characters involved.

Key idea

The rapport that exists between our characters in any interaction should reflect the current mindset of those characters, who they are, and the situation they find themselves in.

Demonstrating rapport between your characters

Rapport is demonstrated in the way people communicate with one another. As we discussed in Chapter 9, only a small part of human communication is through the words we say. Our posture, gestures, facial expressions, voice, skin tone, breathing, proximity and appearance can all send non-verbal signals to other people about what we're thinking and feeling. As people demonstrate their level of rapport with one another through both verbal and non-verbal communication, so should our characters.

It is also important to bear in mind when considering rapport that we begin to read non-verbal signals, such as the clothes people wear and their posture, from the moment we notice them. We also, consciously or subconsciously, make judgements about them from what we see and hear before we interact with them. The rapport-building process does not begin, therefore, when we start a conversation with someone, but when we first become aware of them.

THE DANCE OF CONVERSATION

NLP practitioners often talk about communication being like a dance. When people are in rapport, the conversation flows as if it were a dance performed by talented dancers who know every step by heart. When rapport is lacking, the conversation stumbles and falters as if the dancers are making mistakes, treading on each other's toes or losing the rhythm.

If we watch two people dancing, we will see them move in time with each other, taking turns and **matching** and **mirroring** each other's moves. This is also what happens in a conversation when we are in rapport. We leave spaces for the other person to speak and can match and mirror thoughts, gestures, facial expressions, posture, vocal tones and even the language used. If you go to a public place and watch people interacting with one another, you will see how those strongly engaged in their conversations 'dance' with each other.

Key idea

When people have strong rapport with one another, their interactions can be observed as a dance of words, vocal tones, movement and silences.

People with naturally strong communication skills are likely to subconsciously adjust their verbal and non-verbal responses to match and mirror both the spoken and unspoken communication of others. This helps them build rapport quickly and effectively with strangers. However, NLP considers that these skills can also be learned and improved.

NLP teaches people to build better rapport by encouraging them to learn how to unobtrusively match and mirror other people's verbal and non-verbal signals. A writer does not need to learn to match and mirror themselves, but if they learn to recognize the different ways that people match and mirror, it can help them demonstrate the strength of their characters' rapport to their audience.

MATCHING AND MIRRORING

Non-verbal matching and mirroring can be demonstrated in many ways, e.g. by two people laughing together, sympathetic gestures, matching vocal tones, staring into each other's eyes, expressions that demonstrate one person is listening while the other speaks. See Chapter 9 for more on non-verbal signals.

Try it now

Sit in a public place and, without intruding, watch the conversations going on around you. After a moment or two, instinctively grade each conversation on a rough scale of 1–10 according to how strongly each pair/group of people are in rapport. Now consider their interactions more closely. What are people doing to demonstrate the degree of rapport you perceive?

VERBAL MATCHING AND MIRRORING

Verbal matching and mirroring can be demonstrated by people:

▶ expressing similar beliefs, values and memories

▶ having thinking patterns that are compatible

▶ experiencing similar emotions (although this does not always create rapport)

▶ using the same representational systems (see Chapter 7).

When rapport exists between two people in conversation the words used indicate agreement or a respectful exchange of views. The participants don't question the importance of each other's values or whether what they believe is true, nor do they contradict what the other recollects or feels.

Knowing your characters really well underpins the creation of strong dialogue. After all, it is impossible to divulge a character's beliefs, values, emotions and thought processes through their dialogue if we don't understand what these are. (See Part 1.)

Rapport, however, is not just demonstrated by the thought processes or questions and answers that are evident in our speech. Our language itself can demonstrate we are in rapport.

The depth of the connections we can make through basic spoken language lies on a scale between two extremes. At one extreme is the complete inability to understand someone because they speak a foreign language. At the other extreme, we may use the same dialect, slang, turns of phrase, colloquialisms, etc.

Clearly, the more we share a common vocabulary, the greater the potential for matching and mirroring. The closer the match in the vocabulary we use, the more likely we are to believe, consciously or subconsciously, that we have similar backgrounds, and this helps build rapport.

Beyond the matching and mirroring of language that gives away our background or apparent background, people can also match and mirror the language they use about the topic under discussion and/or their underlying thought processes. For example, people who are afraid may use the language of fear, and quantum physicists will use the language of quantum physics when they talk about quantum physics.

Conversely people can mean the same thing, but use different words to express themselves. In doing so, they may fail to recognize the potential connections that could exist between them. For example, someone may use the word 'intelligent' to mean 'smart' and 'streetwise', but the person they are talking to might think they mean 'academic'.

Try it now

Read through a conversation you have written recently in which two characters who have a lot in common agree with each other. How do they match and mirror each other's words? Could you make them match and mirror more closely and still make their dialogue sound natural?

Don't change anything in your piece, however, unless you feel it adds to your work. Matching and mirroring in dialogue usually needs to be subtle and may or may not suit your style.

REPRESENTATIONAL SYSTEMS AND RAPPORT

As we discussed in Chapter 7, people's preferred representational systems also influence how they interact and communicate with the people around them. Furthermore, although most people aren't aware of it, some of their verbal and non-verbal communication reflects the representational systems they predominantly use. For example, if someone says:

▶ 'That doesn't *look* right to me', it suggests they are using visual processing

▶ 'I don't like the *sound* of that', it suggests they are using auditory processing

▶ 'That doesn't *feel* right to me', it suggests they are using kinaesthetic processing.

If the people in a conversation are predominately using the same representational system, the verbal and non-verbal clues they give relating to this representational system will also naturally match and mirror each other. Having the same preferred representational system therefore tends to help people build rapport more easily, because they have a tendency to process and communicate using the same system.

THE LANGUAGE OF OUR REPRESENTATIONAL SYSTEMS

NLP doesn't take a one-size-fits-all approach to behavioural responses. These tables, therefore, show vocal nuances and body language typical of particular representational systems. However, although a majority of people are likely to behave in this way, not everyone will because of our individual differences. Remember also that while most people have a perceptual preference, unless we are physically incapable of using a particular sense, we all use all representational systems.

Spoken language

Preference	Typical words used	Typical types of phrases used	Typical voice
Visual (seeing)	clear, focus, see, show, recognize, look	'I see what you mean.' 'I can't picture it.' 'I'm in the dark on that one.'	High-pitched and fast
Auditory (hearing)	say, sound, harmony, ask, voice, tune	'I hear what you're saying.' 'He's not speaking my language.' 'It's not ringing any bells with me.'	Clear, precise and medium-paced
Kinaesthetic (feelings and emotions)	handle, touch, impress, grab, move, feel	'Feels good to me.' 'I can't get to grips with it.' 'You've lost me.'	Low, deep and slow with pauses

Unspoken language

Preference	Typical breathing	Typical arm/hand gestures	Typical head position
Visual (seeing)	Shallow and high in the chest	Pointing fingers	Tilted up
Auditory (hearing)	Evenly distributed across the chest	Arms folded	Slightly angled to one side
Kinaesthetic (feelings and emotions)	Deep and low in the stomach	Bent and relaxed	Tipped slightly forward

Try it now

Watch a debate or conversation on television and note the representational language of the speakers when they are in and out of rapport. However, be aware that the representational language of people who are out of rapport may still match if it reflects both speakers' primary representational systems, or the subject under discussion draws them to primarily use a particular representational system.

Remember this

Both the verbal and non-verbal communication we use reflects the representational system we are currently using to process the situation we are in.

CONSIDERING REPRESENTATIONAL SYSTEMS AND YOUR OWN WRITING

When you consider your own work, don't over-analyse every word your characters speak and every gesture they make. Instead, use your understanding of representational systems to ensure that you don't stamp all the dialogue you write with your personal representational preference. Also, if you play up or exaggerate a preference, make sure you have good reason for doing so.

For more information on representational systems and using them in your writing, see Chapters 7 and 8.

Try it now

Using highlighter pens in five different colours, read through a scene you have written and highlight each type of representational preference (visual, auditory, kinaesthetic, olfactory and gustatory) that a character displays – verbally or non-verbally – in a different colour.

Does one colour predominate? Does this demonstrate that you are predominantly assigning a particular representational system to characters?

A WORD OF CAUTION

Only a small percentage of what a writer knows about a character's interactions ever reaches the page. Furthermore, the style of a piece will also dictate what and how a writer demonstrates rapport. It is for you to decide which, if any, key 'observations' about your characters' rapport you wish to show. It is also important not to get too hung up on demonstrating rapport and/or analysing or overworking your writing.

Focus points

The main points to remember from this chapter are:
* Rapport is the degree of harmony, trust, connection and cooperation that exists within a relationship. Strong rapport is demonstrated by people being 'on the same wavelength'. Weak rapport is demonstrated by people who are not communicating well.
* In general, the more we have in common with someone, the stronger our rapport with them is likely to be.
* The rapport a writer demonstrates within any character interaction should reflect the current mindset of the characters, who they are, how they think and the situation they find themselves in.

* When people have strong rapport with each other, their interactions can be observed as a dance of words, vocal tones, movement and silences.
* If writers learn to recognize the different ways that people match and mirror each other's communication, it can help them to demonstrate their characters' rapport to their audience.

Next step

Rapport doesn't just exist between our characters, but also between our story and our audience. Indeed, it is vital to create strong rapport between our audience and our story otherwise the audience will fail to connect and will lose interest in the story. Chapter 11 will consider who your audience is and explore building strong rapport with them.

11

Building strong connections with your audience

In this chapter you will learn about:

▶ *how rapport exists between your audience and your stories*

▶ *ways to build rapport between your audience and your characters*

▶ *ways to build rapport between your audience and your story*

▶ *how hooks, pitches and strong openings create rapport with the people you want to sell your work to and with your audience.*

Self-assessment: How well will your audience connect with your main character?

Answer the following questions about the main character (or one of the main characters) in your work in progress.

1 How old are they?

2 What sex are they?

3 What are their sexual preferences?

4 What do they aspire to achieve?

5 Who are their heroes/role models?

6 What are their values?

7 What beliefs do they hold dear?

8 Do they have a tendency towards certain ways of thinking?

9 Is there an emotional state they regularly find themselves in?

10 What does the audience learn about their past?

Consider these questions again in relation to your intended audience. How many of their answers to the questions would be the same?

In general, the more our audience has in common with a character, the more easily they can build rapport with them and with our story. Therefore, if you found a lot of matches or some very strong matches between your audience and your character, then your character should build strong rapport with your audience. (There are exceptions to this and these will be explored later in this chapter.)

If you don't have an intended audience, this chapter explains the importance of identifying your audience.

It is not just our characters who read one another's spoken and unspoken communication and consciously or subconsciously decide how they feel about one another. Our audience will also process our characters' words and non-verbal signals and decide how they feel about them. The characters in our stories therefore don't just build rapport with one another; they build rapport with our audience. Furthermore, our audience can also be in varying degrees of rapport with our story itself.

Try it now

Consider one of your favourite stories and your favourite character within that story.

- ✲ What beliefs/attitudes do you share with them?
- ✲ What core values do they hold? How many of these are important to you?
- ✲ Is their experience in the story or the back-story similar to anything you have experienced?
- ✲ Is there one 'big thing' that connects you?
- ✲ Do you share a number of recognizable connections?

Your answers should demonstrate that there is a lot of common ground between you. (There are exceptions to this and these will be explored later in this chapter.)

Presupposition: Everyone lives in their own unique model of the world.

The following discussion applies generally to the characters we create and the stories we tell. However, the uniqueness of individuals means that stories and people's reactions to them are exceedingly complex. There will inevitably be exceptions to the 'rules' discussed here. The ideas in this chapter are therefore offered simply as starting points to recognizing how you might be able to build and strengthen your characters' and your story's rapport with your audience.

The presupposition *'Everyone lives in their own unique model of the world'* also tells us that we all perceive and recreate the world in our own unique way. This includes having a unique perception of every story we read or watch. Each audience member will therefore perceive our story in their own way and build their own unique level of rapport with our characters and our story. Inevitably, some people will fail to build strong rapport. If they fail to connect sufficiently, they won't care what happens in our story. If they don't care, they are extremely unlikely to stick it out to the end or recommend it to their friends.

Building rapport between your audience and your story

We writers and our characters are at a disadvantage when building rapport with our audience. Once a book is published or a film made, our characters cannot change how they behave and we cannot change our plot in response to the way our audience reacts; we are completely at their mercy. However, while we are still in the process of writing our story, there is much we can do to influence our audience's reactions and the rapport they build with it and with our characters. The first step is knowing who our audience is.

Key idea

Just as our characters build rapport with one another, our audience also builds rapport with our story and the characters within it. It is therefore imperative that we know who our audience is.

WHAT CREATES RAPPORT BETWEEN YOUR AUDIENCE AND YOUR STORY?

Chapter 10 discussed how rapport between people is dependent on:

▶ their communication skills

▶ the common ground they share

▶ circumstances.

The rapport between our audience and our story is created by the same things. However, in the case of our story:

▶ 'communication skills' means the skill the author has in communicating with their audience

▶ 'common ground' is the common connections between:

▷ the audience and the characters

▷ the audience and the plot

▶ 'circumstances' means the circumstances the characters find themselves in, which are dictated by the plot.

There are therefore three areas which we need to consider when we explore building rapport with our audience:

▶ our writing skills

▶ our characters

▶ our plot.

Case study

In Stephanie Meyer's best-selling novel *Twilight*, teenager Bella Swan falls in love with a vampire, Edward Cullen. Much of *Twilight*'s success is created by the strong rapport Meyer's intended young female audience are encouraged to develop with Bella and with the story itself.

Meyer connects to teenage girls' thinking in the following ways.

✳ Self-perception: Bella is insecure and awkward – a combination anyone who has experienced puberty can identify with.

✳ Teenagers like to live on the edge: Edward's constant fight against his thirst for Bella's blood puts her in great danger. Danger takes us out of our comfort zones and teenagers love pushing boundaries.

✳ Creating the ultimate teenage fantasy man: Edward is described in excruciating detail as an extremely attractive man. Furthermore, he listens to and cares about every word Bella says. He is the fantasy man most teenage girls dream of.

✳ Obsessive detail: when teenage girls develop a crush, they tend to focus on every tiny detail of their idol's appearance, what they say and what they find out about them. Meyer's constant detail about Edward and everything he and Bella say and do together mirrors the way teenage girls in love think about boys and relationships.

✳ Teenage attitudes towards sex: Bella and Edward cannot risk having sex in case Edward loses control and is overtaken by his thirst for Bella's blood. This connects to the dilemma virgin teens often face of yearning for sexual activity, yet being fearful about taking part in it.

Rapport is further encouraged by Bella being described in sparse detail and, as a character, she is relatively lacking in personality. Although many people criticize the book because of this, it enables the teenage reader not just to step into Bella's shoes, but to all but put her on and wear her – allowing them to experience the book on a very personal level.

There is an almost infinite amount to learn about writing and attempting to define what 'writing skills' are would produce an endless list. It is therefore pointless trying to discuss writing skills as a specific topic. Consequently, we will only consider building audience rapport with character and plot in this chapter. However, hopefully this book will help you improve your writing skills, and there are many more books, workshops, courses and other ways to learn to become a better, more skilful writer. However, one important presupposition that impacts on this idea and is worth noting is:

Presupposition: The meaning of a communication is the response you get.

As the author of your story, you are the person responsible for making your communication as clear as possible. Readers or viewers are highly unlikely to consider whether they are misunderstanding you or to spend time trying to understand what you really mean if they perceive things differently from the way you meant them to be understood. Bearing in mind that *'The meaning of a communication is the response you get'* ensures that we recognize why we need to make our communication as clear as possible.

Building strong connections between your audience and your characters

Although audiences build rapport with both plot and character, it is the mental and emotional connections they build with our characters that make them care sufficiently about what happens to them to see the story through to the end. It is imperative, therefore, that our audience builds strong rapport with our main character(s). Ideally, our audience should identify so closely with a main character that they imagine themselves as that person. Unless they feel sufficiently connected and can identify with at least one of the characters, they are unlikely to build strong rapport with our story.

Key idea

If our audience fails to connect with the very person/people that a story is about, they won't care what happens to them and are unlikely to enjoy the story or see it through to the end.

Leaving aside writing skills, the rapport our characters create with our audience is influenced by the common ground they share, or the lack of it. For a character to build rapport with our audience, our audience needs to:

▶ share some of the same or similar beliefs

▶ have shared memories or a common past

▶ share some of the same or similar values

▶ be familiar with the same or similar emotional state(s) as those displayed by the character

▶ have some of the same or similar thinking patterns.

Our audience does not have to connect on every level with every character to have good rapport with them or with our story. However, just as when real people build rapport with one another, the greater the number of connections an audience makes with a character, the better the rapport they are likely to build. Therefore we usually want our protagonist to make plenty of strong connections with our audience.

Try it now

Consider the main character (or one of the main characters) of your work in progress and the audience your story is intended for.

✳ What beliefs do they have in common?

✳ What values do they share?

✳ What past experiences, or similar past experiences, do they share?

✳ Are they often in similar emotional states or do they have people close to them who are?

✳ What similarities are there between the ways they think?

Key idea

There needs to be sufficient common ground between a character and our intended audience for strong connections to be made between them and therefore strong rapport to develop between them.

CONSIDERING YOUR WHOLE CAST

Although we should usually aim to create the strongest rapport between our main character(s) and our audience, our audience needs to have a degree of rapport with all our characters. An absence of rapport means an absence of connection and if our audience fails to connect to a character, at least in some way, this tends to leave the character seeming two-dimensional.

Even when we are creating 'bad guys', our audience needs to connect with them in some way to understand the place inside them that their motivation comes from. This doesn't mean the audience has to like that part of them, but it needs to recognize the character's core as belonging to a real human being.

It is also important not just to look at your characters in isolation. It is the combination of characters along with the plot they exist in that generates the level of rapport your audience builds with your whole story. For example, most stories will benefit from having a proactive primary character, but, as discussed in the case study above, Bella Swan in *Twilight* lacks proactivity. In this case, Bella's lack of proactivity is a positive in building rapport, because the audience develops stronger rapport with the story by spending time with Edward than by identifying with what Bella achieves. Getting the mixture and balance of characters right is paramount; you wouldn't put a straight man on stage without his comedian, Winnie-the-Pooh would be far poorer without Eeyore, and where would Sherlock Holmes be without Watson?

EXPLORING COMMON GROUND

▶ Beliefs and memories

Whether our audience makes sufficient connection with our characters' beliefs and memories is usually straightforward; they will recognize (on a conscious or subconscious level) either that they do or that they don't.

Remember this

In order for rapport to build between our audience and our characters, our audience needs to recognize the connections they have with the characters on either a conscious or a subconscious level. These connections therefore need to turn up in some form on the page, not just be buried in your character portraits.

▶ Core values

When our core values are at odds with someone else's, we find it hard to get on with them because our values are at the very heart of who we are. Identifying our audience's likely core values and giving some of these values to our main character(s) can be a good way to build strong rapport between the audience and the main character. Equally, creating a character who acts against one or more of our audience's core values is a good way to influence the audience to dislike them.

▶ Common values

While we all have our own unique set of core values, there are common values, such as fairness and respect, which most people admire, even if they find it hard to uphold these values themselves. Giving a character some of these values will help build rapport with most people.

▶ Understanding values

We usually have to create characters that our audience dislikes as well as loves. If 'unlikeable' characters are to feel real to our audience, we need the audience to understand the character's motivation and possibly build a sympathetic connection with them. Values can be an important tool for establishing rapport with unlikeable characters. If a character upholds even a single core value that our audience shares, this can create understanding and build some degree of rapport between them, even if they are upholding that value in a way our audience doesn't agree with.

▶ Stimulating values

Sometimes a character can stimulate values that we hold. When the value is stimulated, we make a connection to the character or at least to the story. For example, although on paper we may have nothing in common with a serial killer, we may value curiosity or inquisitiveness and this value might be stimulated by our interest in why they behave the way they do and/or how they manage to evade detection.

▶ Projection

Our audience doesn't have to have experienced a situation themselves to 'know' how a character feels. People project memories of their own experiences onto the situations they see as similar. This allows our audience to imagine themselves in the same situations as our characters despite never having encountered these themselves. For example, when Oliver Twist asks for more to eat, we don't have to have been an orphan growing up in a 19th-century poorhouse to imagine how Oliver feels. We've all been hungry. We've all experienced peer pressure. We've all been children afraid to say something to a scary grown-up. We can therefore project ourselves into Oliver's shoes and imagine what it's like for him to be the one chosen to stand up to Mr Bumble.

▶ Emotion

The emotional reactions we evoke in our audience often have a greater impact on rapport than the intellectual reactions. This is because when people have an emotional reaction they don't need to process the connection they are making – they instantly 'know' they feel that way and understand the way the character feels. Creating rapport through the emotional state we develop in our audience can therefore be highly effective.

Surprisingly, prompting negative emotions in our audience can be as helpful, and sometimes more helpful, in building rapport than prompting positive emotions. This is because our audience can engage with the negative feelings – for example, fear, shock or disgust – both by experiencing the emotions themselves and by recognizing that the character is feeling these emotions and empathizing with them. This creates two ways for the audience to connect to the character/story.

▶ If they care sufficiently about the character, they will be concerned for them.

▶ Whether they are concerned for the character or not, they are likely to be subconsciously processing how they would feel in the same situation and keen to discover the character's outcome within the situation for the sake of their own sense of wellbeing.

▶ Characters we love to hate

We've all met characters that we truly enjoyed seeing get their comeuppance. Building a strong negative emotional relationship between your audience and one or more of your characters:

▶ makes your audience feel good, because they are championing not just the 'good' character(s) but also the side of 'goodness and truth' – or whatever you might call it. This brings us back to the idea of common values that most people aspire to, because when we root against the 'bad guy' we feel as if we are honouring values we admire.

▶ provides true satisfaction when the 'good guy' wins – again, this links to the common values that we admire being upheld and satisfied.

▶ Proactiveness

Just as we can have values that we aspire to but don't always uphold as well as we'd like to, so we can also aspire to think and behave in certain ways that we rarely or never do.

Even if someone isn't particularly proactive in their own life, they are unlikely to be interested in or to connect strongly to a protagonist who fails to be proactive. This is because:

▶ even a strong character becomes boring if they wait for others to take the lead, or for life to come to them

▶ most people tend to imagine themselves in the protagonist's shoes. If the protagonist isn't 'in charge' of the forward movement of the story, then the audience won't share any real experience with them.

▶ Thinking patterns

Sometimes a connection is built between our audience and a character because:

- they share the same ways of thinking

- their thinking patterns are not the same, but our audience admires or aspires to thinking in the way our characters do

- our audience might like to think that they would have the same thinking patterns as our character displays in the situations our story puts them in.

Thinking patterns are therefore more complex and story-dependent, because we read stories in order to engage with the characters, but different stories lead us to engage differently. For example, we may recognize and connect with Piglet's anxieties when we read *Winnie-the-Pooh* because we have had similar anxieties ourselves, but when we watch a James Bond film, we may see ourselves as 007 because it allows us to explore and try on a character we are never likely to be. The result is that sometimes we connect with thinking patterns that we share with a character, and at other times we connect with thinking patterns that are dissimilar to our own in order to experience or explore being someone else, or to experience a situation we are unlikely to ever be in.

Humour

Our sense of humour is based on a near-indefinable set of beliefs about what is amusing. When we find something funny, we make a strong connection to a story and/or the character who made us laugh. The connection lies in having the same sense of humour and, at the same time, also experiencing the emotions of being amused. Even if we're not writing a humorous book, a few laughs in appropriate places can work wonders in cementing an audience's connection with our story, our authorial voice and/or our characters.

Simple connections

Don't overlook the simple connections your audience can make with your story, such as being the same age as the protagonist. Remember, however, that simple things can also turn people off if they don't share the connection; for example if a character is a smoker.

▶ Denial

Sometimes people refuse, consciously or subconsciously, to believe certain things about themselves or about what they do. This can range from beliefs that are unlikely to have significant consequences – such as thinking they are the best player in their amateur football team – to the serious – such as being in denial about abuse they experienced as a child.

Because we are able to lie, even to ourselves, about our beliefs, values, memories, experiences, emotions and the way we think, we may be unable to recognize the common ground we have with some characters. Furthermore, we may be so far in denial that we react adversely to a character that we have a lot in common with, because thinking about them pushes us too far out of our comfort zone.

Remember this

We are all unique. Different people will build different degrees of rapport with our characters. Some of our audience may even build greater rapport with the less important characters than the main characters. However, while differences are inevitable, what's important is to understand our core audience and build a strong rapport with them.

Using plot to create strong connections with your audience

We all have favourite types of stories that engage us while others leave us cold. For instance, one person may love romantic comedies and another may find them tedious. We develop favourites because similar genres and types of story have similarities in their content, and it is these similarities that we love to connect to.

Recognizing which elements of our plot may excite and interest our audience can help us to strengthen the connections those elements make with the audience. There are generally two types of connection our audience makes:

▶ to elements of the plot; for example, our audience may feel exhilaration when they become engaged in a chase scene

▶ to a type of character that inhabits a particular type of story; for example, the underdog plot requires an underdog character who, if he/she is to win the day, requires particular qualities and values, such as persistence, determination and resourcefulness.

We can therefore increase our audience's rapport with our story type by ensuring that:

▶ we include the elements and plot devices that our audience wants and expects from that type of story

▶ we give our characters the values, qualities, background and/or behaviours that are expected of that genre, and then increase the emotion in those connections between the audience and main character(s) by tweaking the elements and plot devices that belong to that type of story. For example, stacking the odds higher and higher against the underdog, keeping the lovers apart for longer, hiding the treasure in a seemingly inaccessible place.

Try it now

✻ What type of story is your work in progress? Remember, stories can be a mixture of types. For example, a ghost story in which the ghost seeks revenge is both a ghost story and a revenge plot.

✻ What are the essential plot elements and character types that inhabit your story type(s)?

✻ How does your audience connect to these elements/characters on an emotional level? For example, in a ghost story the emotions include tension and fear.

✻ How can you tweak your plot to increase these emotions in your audience?

Key idea

Plot elements can be developed to increase rapport between the audience and the story or characters.

Remember this

Trotting out the same old characters in the same old genre won't excite your potential audience and therefore publishers or film-makers won't be interested in taking on your novel or script if they've seen it all before. Alongside considering how to create audience rapport, we need to ensure there is originality in our characters and in how the plot 'treats' them.

Hooks and pitches

As discussed in Chapter 10, we begin to build (or fail to build) rapport with other people the moment we first see them. The same applies to our stories; our audience starts out knowing nothing about them and having zero rapport with them. Similarly, rapport can grow or be eroded, or opportunities to build rapport can be lost, before a book is opened or a film even starts.

The rapport-building process for a book or film is kicked off by any public relations or marketing activity and/or by the blurb on the cover of your book or DVD. The content of these may be decided by your publicity department and may therefore seem beyond your control. However, these elements start off within your control when you write a pitch for your story.

Creating a pitch for your story is important because it:

▶ initially helps others to become interested in and excited by your work

▶ may be used or modified by those who market your work.

Hooks and pitches work by creating an instant connection and understanding. The 1979 film *Alien* was famously pitched as '*Jaws* in space'. This created an easy understanding of what the film was about in only three words. It also allowed the potential audience to work out whether they were interested and excited by the idea. Creating interest and excitement are important because interest generates an intellectual connection and excitement an emotional connection with the idea. These connections kick off the rapport-building process. Being bored by an idea prevents a connection being made and rapport being built.

Case study

The pitch '*Jaws* in space' is essentially a very brief plot explanation. (Although it also tell us that one of the characters is a highly efficient killing machine that can't be reasoned with.) In 1979, when nobody had seen the film *Alien*, we might have been hooked by this pitch because we:

* found it exciting to watch a suspenseful 'monster in the shadows' type horror plot
* valued experiencing fear and excitement
* loved to be scared in a safe environment
* framed *Jaws* as a great movie.

Others might have failed to be hooked because they:

* found it dull to watch a suspenseful 'monster in the shadows' type horror plot
* valued reality and considered this sort of escapist film a waste of time
* didn't enjoy horror
* framed *Jaws* as an awful movie.

These are just a few examples of how the pitch '*Jaws* in space' might have created a connection with the film's potential audience; There will have been other reasons that people might or might not connect to a plot described in this way.

Try it now

* What genre(s) or type(s) of story are you currently writing?
* What are your story's hooks and unique selling points?
* What is special about your story?

Write a paragraph explaining your story in terms of genre, hook and unique selling points. When you have done this, hone the paragraph down to one or two enticing lines that encapsulate why people will want to read or watch your story.

As an alternative or in addition, create a movie-style pitch by considering which combination of books, films or genres your story resembles.

Opening rapport

One strong connection is sometimes all that is needed to build strong rapport. This is the reason many books, television dramas and films start off with:

▶ a 'big' scene that epitomizes the type of story that is going to be told; for example, a horror story may start with a really gruesome event

▶ a scene that builds rapport with a major character; for example, Pip's encounter with Magwitch in the graveyard at the start of Dickens' *Great Expectations*.

Although a 'big' scene can help in building strong connections quickly, the rapport must be maintained. Many new writers make the mistake of starting with a big scene and then writing chapter after chapter of dull story or back-story, or even writing a completely different story or characters to the one(s) the opening scene(s) promised.

Try it now

Read the first chapter or opening scenes of your work in progress and answer the following questions.

✳ What sort of story does it seem as if this opening is introducing?
✳ How representative of the rest of the story is this opening?
✳ What does this opening promise the reader?
✳ Does the rest of your story deliver this/these promise(s)?
✳ How does this opening connect your audience to your story?
✳ How does this opening connect your audience to your main character(s)?

Key idea

It is vital to build good rapport between our story and our audience as quickly and as effectively as possible.

THE FIRST CHARACTERS OUR AUDIENCE MEETS

Audiences tend to assume that the characters they meet in the opening scene(s) of a story are the main characters. If this isn't the case, it can interfere with the rapport-building process, because the audience usually begins to subconsciously assess and build rapport with the first characters they meet in the belief that they are the main characters. If the main characters appear later, the audience has to start building rapport once more, thus slowing down the rapport-building process with the story. Some people may also feel cheated if they were building a good rapport with the initial characters only for them to vanish from the story or turn out to have insignificant roles.

There are, however, exceptions; it is acceptable to start a story with people who aren't the main character(s) in, for example, a detective story where someone is murdered at the start. This works because it meets the audience's expectation of this genre, and because in crime fiction the victim's presence will remain throughout the story as their murder is investigated.

Audiences usually understand genres where it is acceptable to start without the main character(s) in the opening scene, and this understanding means the rapport-building process is not troubled. However, in general, it is advisable for at least some of your main characters to be the first characters your audience meets.

You can't please all the people all the time

As a writers, we are not in control of our audience and there will always be people who don't understand or connect with our work. There is therefore no point expecting to connect to everyone, or everyone we see as our target audience. People are too complex for any writer to be able to do that. Instead, what we should aim for is to understand the audience we are writing for and understand what is likely to build or destroy rapport with them.

It is not just the make-up of a person that causes them to connect or fail to connect to our story. If someone is not receptive to our ideas or writing style, or is not in a mood conducive to connecting with our story, they won't build rapport with our work – even if they would when they were in a more receptive frame of mind.

Focus points

The main points to remember from this chapter are:

✳ Just as our characters build rapport with one another, so our audience builds rapport with our stories and the characters in them. It is therefore imperative that we know who our audience is.

✳ If our audience fails to connect to the very person/people a story is about, they won't care what happens to them. If they don't care what happens to our characters, they are extremely unlikely to stick with our story to the end or recommend it to their friends.

✳ There needs to be sufficient common ground between our main character(s) and our intended audience for strong connections to be made and therefore strong rapport to be created.

✳ Plot elements can be tweaked to increase rapport between the audience and the story and characters.

✳ It is vital to build rapport between our story and our audience as quickly and as effectively as possible.

Next step

In Chapter 12, we will consider further the plots of our stories and how NLP's idea of *well-formed outcomes* can be used to explore and improve our plots.

Part 4

Plotting and perspective

12

Developing and improving your plot

In this chapter you will learn about:

▶ *goals, outcomes and well-formed outcomes*
▶ *how the conditions of well-formed outcomes can be used to improve your plots.*

Self-assessment: How well paced is your story

List the chapter numbers of your work in progress, from 1 to however many chapters your story has; if you are a scriptwriter, number the scenes and make a list of the scene numbers. If you haven't completed a first draft, define your chapters/scenes by the main events that happen in the story. If there are gaps in your plot, just write 'something happens here' and count it as a chapter/scene.

Next to each chapter/scene, add 'H' if it includes a high in the action and 'B' if it takes a break from the action. If a scene or chapter includes both a high in the action and a break of significant length, note 'H, B' or 'B, H', depending on the order they occur. Total up how many H's and B's there are altogether.

Draw two horizontal straight lines, parallel with each other. Label the top one 'H' and the bottom 'B'. Mark the bottom line with the same number of markers as your total number of H's plus B's.

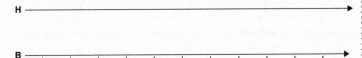

Plot your high action (H) and breaks in the action (B) on the parallel lines. For example if your list is H, B, B, H, B, H, H, B, B, B, B, it would look like this:

Join the points between the two lines to form a graph. If you did this for the list in the example above, it would look like this:

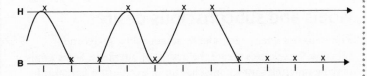

This graph shows the rise and fall in the action of your story. Ideally there should be a regular rise and fall in your graph demonstrating that the action peaks and troughs, thus maintaining your audience's interest but giving them time to breathe between the action.

Slow and 'soggy' patches occur in a story if the break from high action lasts too long. However, if the high action lasts too long without giving your audience a break, it can make your work feel tedious too. In the example here, the drop at the end of the graph would suggest that the story ending is too flat.

When you consider your graph, bear in mind also that, while audiences need a little time to catch their breath, different genres require different pacing – so there's no one rule of thumb about how long high action should go on for or how long your audience needs a break from it.

Your graph should help you to identify areas where you might need to work on the pacing of your plot. However, if you are not familiar with the pacing of the genre you are writing in, it is important to familiarize yourself with work that is typical of the genre so that you understand the pacing required; then compare your graph with this.

When considering the structure of a story, remember too that stories also require an emotional storyline. The emotional storyline charts how the action storyline affects the main character and therefore also rises and falls in a reflection of the highs and lows of the action storyline.

Key idea

Stories require a constant rise and fall in tension both in the action storyline and the emotional storyline.

Goals and subconscious desires

The steps our characters take to achieve their goals and subconscious desires create the action of our story. Some goals may be only relevant to one chapter or even just a paragraph or two. For example, in the story *The Three Little Pigs*, the Big Bad Wolf's goal of blowing down the house made of straw lasts only until he blows it down, and then he moves on to his next goal: to catch the first little pig. However, some goals span the entire story. For example, throughout the story, the Big Bad Wolf works toward his goal (which he ultimately fails to achieve) of eating all three little pigs.

Characters are always working towards achieving something. However, a character does not have to consciously set out or work towards an outcome. They can begin to work towards a goal at any point in a story, work towards one unconsciously or achieve a final outcome they were never working towards.

Try it now

Read a chapter of a book you have read before and identify what goals each character is working towards in that chapter. Consider both the story's overarching goal(s) and the more immediate goals of the characters, some of which may be stepping stones to achieving the overarching goals. For instance, in *The Three Little Pigs* example mentioned above, the Big Bad Wolf's immediate goals of blowing down the first little pig's house and catching the first little pig are also part of his overarching goal of eating all three little pigs.

Key idea

Characters are always working towards achieving something.

OUTCOMES

In NLP, **outcome** means 'what we get as a result of our actions'. This term is used in preference to 'goal' because NLP practitioners consider that a goal is something we want, while an outcome is what we get. This distinction can seem rather pedantic and make discussion of what our characters are striving to achieve confusing. So for the purposes of this book, it doesn't matter whether you think of what a character is working towards achieving as a goal or as an outcome.

Although adding the term 'outcome' to our discussions may seem to overcomplicate things, considering some elements of NLP's method of focusing on what people want (or need) to achieve can be helpful.

NLP's method of focusing on what people want (or need) to achieve is called **well-formed outcomes**. Well-formed outcomes are a very precise and structured approach to planning achievement that fits nine conditions which are designed to increase the likelihood of success.

The nine conditions that make up a well-formed outcome are that the person embarking on achieving the outcome:

1 understands the consequences of achieving the outcome

2 ensures the outcome preserves existing benefits

3 knows how they will 'measure' their success

4 has access to resources

5 considers the context

6 is as specific as possible about what they want to achieve

7 states the outcome they want in positive terms

8 has an action plan

9 is in control of the outcome.

Key idea

Well-formed outcomes is a method of achieving an outcome that fits nine specific conditions. Considering some of these conditions in relation to our writing can help us consider and improve our plots.

USING WELL-FORMED OUTCOMES TO IMPROVE YOUR PLOT

Just as with any device designed to help improve our writing, using well-formed outcomes needs to be employed at the right time and in the right way. If you're happily writing or growing a story in your head, interrupting your creative process may detract from it. Therefore, this method is best used if you are:

- new to plotting and need a method to help you work on your plot
- experiencing plot challenges
- at the revision stage, having completed a first full draft.

The main areas the conditions of well-formed outcomes can help you work on are:

- ensuring your plotting/structure is sound
- sorting out a plot that isn't working
- working out how your characters succeed or fail
- working out why your characters succeed or fail
- adding subplots or plot twists
- adding conflict and tension
- removing slow and 'soggy' patches
- developing your plot
- ensuring events unfold and impact logically on each character.

What do your characters want to achieve?

To make the best use of well-formed outcomes in working on our plot, we need to create an overview of what our characters want to achieve.

Try it now

The following questions will help you explore your plot in terms of your characters' primary wants and needs and the outcomes they achieve.

Consider each significant character separately and ask yourself the following questions.

When my audience first meets this character:

* what does this character want most in all the world?

* what is this character running away from?
* what does this character need? (They may realize this, may not realize this yet or may never realize it.)
* What is this character's primary goal within the story?
* Does what this character primarily wants change during the story? If so, what new outcomes do they strive to achieve?
* Does this character get what they most want? If not, why not?
* Does this character get what they need? If not, why not?

Remember this

Characters don't have to be consciously aware of having goals, but as a writer you must know what goal each character is working towards achieving at any point that the focus is on them – both in terms of what they want/need to achieve at that point in the story and their primary/ overall goal(s) in the story. Once you have a clearer picture of the main goals your characters are striving to achieve, you can use the nine conditions of well-formed outcomes in the ways suggested below to revise your work or to develop your plot.

THE NINE CONDITIONS

In NLP, the well-formed outcomes' conditions are considered when people are planning work on an achievement and they want to:

▶ maximize their chances of success

▶ make the journey towards success as smooth and swift as possible.

When writers develop a story, they usually:

▶ want to minimize the chances of success of characters the audience is rooting for until the end of the story

▶ don't want their characters to move too quickly from the start of the story to the finish.

If a writer is still developing their story, they also usually don't want to pin down too tightly what their characters accomplish, or their creativity and the development of their story could be smothered.

If a writer is revising their story or has their plot already worked out, they may be considering the well-formed outcomes' conditions in a retrospective manner, already knowing precisely what the character finally accomplishes.

Because of these considerations, the following four conditions are of little use to the writer

▶ Be as specific as possible about what you want to achieve.

▶ State the outcome you want in positive terms.

▶ Have an action plan.

▶ Be in control of the outcome.

The remaining five conditions can, however, be helpful and we will now explore their usefulness.

The consequences of your characters' actions

Presupposition: Life, mind and body are one system.

This presupposition tells us that everything we do impacts on ourselves, our environment and everyone around us. The two conditions of well-formed outcomes that acknowledge this are:

1 *Understand the consequences of achieving the outcome*, i.e. consider the impact your actions towards achieving your outcome will have on you, on others and on your environment

2 *Ensure the outcome preserves existing benefits*, i.e. ensure the actions you take don't remove any positives you already have.

Both these conditions direct us to ensure we understand and consider the consequences of our actions. This is a very important point for writers to focus on, because every story requires an inner logic of cause and effect, i.e. characters take actions initiated by the inciting incident, and these actions have consequences. As a result of those consequences the characters take further actions, which then have further consequences, and so on. The story therefore progresses as a chain of cause and effect arising from the characters reacting to the consequences of their own and one another's previous actions.

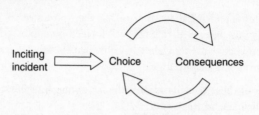

Inciting incident ⟶ Choice ↻ Consequences

Case study

Consider how the meeting of Rose DeWitt Bukater and Jack Dawson in the film *Titanic* sets off a chain of cause and effect of characters reacting to the consequences of their own and one another's actions.

Rose, a first-class passenger, boards the *Titanic* with her fiancé Cal. Her marriage to him will solve the DeWitt Bukaters' financial problems. But Rose is so distraught at the idea of marrying Cal that she goes to the ship's stern intending to kill herself by jumping overboard.

Consequence: Jack finds Rose and stops her.

Consequence: Rose and Jack form a friendship which develops into mutual attraction and they meet in secret.

Consequence: Cal finds out and forbids Rose from seeing Jack.

Consequence: Rose complies with Cal's orders.

Consequence: Jack tries to make Rose face up to the realities of married life with Cal.

Consequence: Rose realizes Jack is right and that she is no longer prepared to allow Cal and her mother to control her.

Consequence: To demonstrate her defiance, Rose asks Jack to sketch her wearing only a rare diamond necklace Cal has given her. She places the picture in Cal's safe, along with the necklace and a mocking note.

Consequence: Cal is furious and frames Jack for stealing the necklace.

Consequence: Jack is arrested and handcuffed to a pipe in the master-at-arms' office.

At this point the *Titanic*'s story collides with Rose and Jack's story, as the ship is now sinking.

Consequence: Cal and Rose head for the lifeboats, but on the way Rose learns that Jack is trapped.

Consequence: Rose leaves Cal and frees Jack.

Consequence: Cal tries to reclaim Rose by putting her on a lifeboat and leaving Jack onboard.

Consequence: Already knowing there aren't enough lifeboats, Rose realizes Jack can't escape and that she cannot leave him to die alone, so jumps back onboard.

Consequence: Cal is incensed. Determined not to let Jack 'win', he tries to shoot Jack, but fails.

Consequence: Cal realizes he has lost and leaves Jack and Rose to take their chances on the sinking ship.

CAUSE AND EFFECT

Whether we are creating a new plot, developing an existing one or reflecting on our plot structure, we can use the idea of our characters' actions having consequences to check that our plot is driven by a chain of cause and effect (i.e. created by characters reacting to the consequences of their own and one another's actions).

Try it now

Consider the storyline you are currently working on.

* Do the main events of each plot strand occur in a logical sequence of cause and effect generated by the consequences of the choices the character makes and the actions they take?
* Are you acknowledging the impact **all** your characters' actions have on one another?
* Are you acknowledging the impact **all** the plot strands have on one another?

WORST POSSIBLE CONSEQUENCES

Stories thrive on our characters facing challenges and conflict, not on their lives running smoothly. When the consequences of our characters' actions create additional challenges for them or for other characters, we build further excitement and interest. Tension is also created when our characters are taken further away from the goals they want or need to achieve.

Understanding the consequences of our characters' actions can therefore be used in the opposite way to how NLP intends it to be used, i.e. we can ensure our character's actions:

▶ have the worst possible consequences, rather than aiming for them to have the best possible consequences

▶ take our characters further away from their goals rather than towards them.

Uncle Vernon recognizes that the Hogwarts' letter is from the magical world, so snatches it away before Harry can open it. As a result, Hogwarts send a second letter the next day. Once more Uncle Vernon refuses to let Harry have it.

On the third day, three letters arrive. Uncle Vernon destroys them and nails up the letterbox.

On the fourth day, 12 letters are shoved through the cracks around the door. Uncle Vernon burns the letters and boards up the cracks.

On the fifth day, 24 letters arrive, hidden in two dozen eggs. Aunt Petunia shreds the letters, but the next day letters stream down the chimney.

Desperate to keep Harry from reading the letters, Uncle Vernon takes the family to a hotel, but the next morning hundreds of letters arrive for Harry.

So Uncle Vernon scours the country for somewhere the letters can't find them. The family ends up in a shack on a rock in the middle of the sea. But in the morning – the dawn of Harry's 11th birthday – Hagrid arrives on a flying motorbike and personally hands a letter to Harry.

Key idea

Every action our characters take has consequences that impact on them, other characters and their environment.

▶ Developing your current plot by considering the worst possible consequences

When we create a story, we may instinctively develop a chain of cause and effect that is perfect for the overall story. However, sometimes we know what we want our characters to achieve but are not sure of all the steps to get them there. At other times we have the steps in place but the story lacks sufficient excitement, conflict, tension or depth. Reflecting on the potential consequences of the action(s) our characters take can help fill in gaps in our plot, remove the 'soggy' patches and make our story shine.

1 If you are at a point where one of your main characters takes action or needs to take action but subsequently the plots flags, or you don't know what action they should take, ask:

   ▷ what does this character need/want to achieve at this point?

   ▷ what action (if any) do they currently take to accomplish this?

2 Next, brainstorm all the different actions the character(s) could take at this point – including doing nothing.

3 Once you have a list of possible actions, identify which of these actions are consistent with the character's values and beliefs. (See Chapters 1 and 2.)

4 Write each of the actions that are consistent with this character's values and beliefs at the top of separate pieces of paper. For each action, identify as many answers as possible to the following questions and write your answers on that action's piece of paper. If my character took this action:

   ▷ what could they lose?

   ▷ what could they gain?

   ▷ what could prevent them carrying out this action?

   ▷ what result(s) will take them towards their current goal?

   ▷ what result(s) will take them away from their current goal?

   ▷ what result(s) would take them towards their overarching story goal(s)?

   ▷ what result(s) would take them away from their overarching story goal(s)?

   ▷ what impact could this action have on each of the other characters?

   ▷ how could each of the other characters react to this impact?

   ▷ what could be the consequences for their world in general?

Use the answers you come up with to generate new directions that your plot could take and/or to identify how you can maximize the conflict or increase tension within a 'soggy' part of your story.

Remember this

When we work to improve a story by considering the possible consequences of our characters' actions, we can look at everything – from a single event in a story and the tiniest ripples it creates, up to the main events in the overall plot.

▶ Developing a new plot by considering the worst possible consequences

Sometimes writers only have the start of an idea for a story or a character or two in their head. If this is the case for you, try using the exercise above to brainstorm ideas that you can develop into a story in one of the following ways.

1 If you have identified an inciting incident, kick-start your creative processes by brainstorming how your main character could react to the inciting incident, i.e. all the possible actions they could take. Once you have a list of possible actions, use the questions in part 4 of the exercise to explore the possibilities of what could happen next.

Your own creative instincts may take over as you work on this exercise, but if you come to the end and feel you need more help, identify the reaction to the inciting incident that most appeals to you. Taking the possible consequences of that action one by one, use parts 2–4 in the exercise to identify the possible actions the main character might take in response and the possible subsequent consequences. Hopefully your creative instincts will kick in during this process and you will be able to build your story without further interrogation and brainstorming. If your creative instincts haven't kicked in by now, it's probably time to ask if your initial idea or characters currently excite you enough for them to be turned into a story.

2 If you don't have an inciting incident, ask what is the worst thing that could happen to this character in the situation they are currently in? Brainstorm this question. Identify the most appealing possibility from your brainstorming. Use this as your inciting incident and develop your plot as explained above.

GETTING THE TENSION BALANCE RIGHT

While tension is often built by preventing the characters our audience is rooting for from achieving what they want or need to achieve, there is a limit to the length of time and the number of times we should do this. Interest and tension can only be held for so long before an audience:

▶ grows bored, or

▶ feels it is unrealistic that the character(s) would keep striving towards the goal, or

▶ feels characters must be real losers not to get it right at least occasionally, or

▶ feels they are being 'strung along'.

The characters you want your audience to side with must therefore win at least small victories and not constantly be the loser in all interactions. However, characters like Uncle Vernon and Aunt Petunia, who are effectively 'comedy characters' and who your audience should be rooting against, can get it wrong every time.

The overall tension also needs to arise from within a story. Once a key character that our audience is rooting for overcomes a challenge, presenting the character with a lesser challenge is pointless because the audience will already believe the character can overcome it. Writers therefore usually have to make the character's life even tougher, their goals even harder to achieve, or take them further away from what they want/need to achieve until the very end of the story – with the proviso, of course, that these characters should usually win at least some small victories.

Remember this

When your characters' strategies fail, lead them away from their true goal or lead them on to harder challenges, this builds tension and keeps your audience turning the pages or glued to the screen.

REFLECTING ON YOUR PLOT STRUCTURE

As you construct your plot and when you revise your work, take a minute or two regularly to check whether your plot is working hard enough. If it isn't, consider how you could use the idea of worst possible consequences to create greater challenges for your characters.

Measuring your characters' success

Condition 3 of the nine conditions of well-formed outcomes states that we need to know how we will measure our success. If we don't, we may not recognize whether or not we have succeeded in achieving the outcome we were aiming for. NLP therefore encourages people to identify how they can measure their success.

While a character doesn't always have to know they have achieved an outcome, the author must demonstrate to their audience what outcome(s) their characters have achieved. Otherwise the story will lack a satisfying ending and/or the intentions of the author may be misunderstood by the audience. Writers therefore need to know how their characters' achievements can be measured and recognized by the audience.

Sometimes it is easy to place measures on outcomes and demonstrate change to our audience; it's easy enough to show that the factory owner has turned his business around, that the long-lost son has returned home or that the beautician from Albuquerque has wiped out the invading aliens. However other changes, particularly emotional ones, can be harder to demonstrate. In particular, it can be easy – especially for beginner writers – to assume the audience understands the way a character feels, because that's how the author believes they would feel after the experiences of the story.

Try it now

If you're struggling to find measures to demonstrate a change in your story, try asking the following questions.

* What will the character(s) be able to do differently when this change has occurred?

* What will the character(s) see, hear and feel when this change has occurred?
* What will the audience or other characters notice is different?
* What will the character(s) have gained that they didn't have before?
* How have the character(s) lives improved?
* How have the character(s) lives become worse?

SHOW, DON'T TELL

When you write about emotional/internal changes, always remember the old adage, 'Show, don't tell'. Allow your character(s) to demonstrate the changes that have occurred through the actions they take, rather than directly stating these through their dialogue or in a narrative explanation.

Having the right resources

Condition 4 of the nine conditions of well-formed outcomes states that we need access to resources. In other words, people need to have the right skills, knowledge and physical resources to achieve their desired outcome(s). As writers, we need to ensure our characters have the skills, knowledge and physical resources they require to achieve the outcomes they achieve.

In real life, it can take time to acquire both physical resources and the skills we require. In fiction, the writer has the power to change the back-story of a character or alter the plot to ensure a character has what they need when they need it. However, when we equip our characters with their requirements, we need to ensure this feels congruent to the audience.

ENSURING CONGRUENCE

▶ Foreshadowing

If characters apparently acquire knowledge, skills or physical objects from nowhere, our audience is likely to feel cheated and both our characters and our plot become less believable. If your character needs to know the antidote to an ancient Egyptian curse, be able to perform a complex martial art or possess a haunted mirror, don't just spring the possession of this on your audience. Demonstrate early in the story that your character has, or is likely to have, an ability or own a possession they require later in the plot. However, remember you don't have to write the whole story of your character's life in Egypt, or their kung fu training or how they came to own the haunted mirror. Unless it's necessary to the story to show more – or you realize it would improve your story to show more – you only need to drop a few clues or place a few pointers to foreshadow a character's possession of the resources they need.

▶ Magic changes

As you work on or revise your plot, it's worth checking that your characters haven't experienced any 'magic changes'. For example, if the trolls failed to storm the castle the first time, something needs to change if they are to break in at the second attempt. If the boss doesn't trust her PA with the keys to the safe in Chapter 3, something needs to change if she's going to trust the PA with them in Chapter 8. This might sound obvious, but it is easy for this sort of error to creep in as plots grow and change.

Considering the context

Condition 5 of the nine conditions of well-formed outcomes states that we need to consider the context. This condition tells people to check whether they want to make the changes they have identified in all areas of their lives or if the change is appropriate only in certain circumstances. Usually this condition applies to people making behavioural changes, where it may be fitting to behave in a certain way in one situation but not in another.

The idea of context applies to our characters too, because we want our audience to believe our characters are real people. We therefore need to make sure they behave in ways appropriate to the situations they find themselves in. This doesn't mean that they have to behave with perfect social etiquette in every situation they encounter, but they must behave in a way that is consistent with the character you have created for them.

Focus points

The main points to remember from this chapter are:

✽ Our characters are constantly working to achieve their goals; they don't need to be consciously aware of them, but you do.

✽ Well-formed outcomes is a method of achieving an outcome that fits nine specific conditions. Considering some of these conditions in relation to our writing can help us consider and improve our plots.

✽ Our characters' actions have consequences and the consequences of their actions build the chain of cause and effect that logical plotting requires.

✽ Placing measures on our characters' achievements allows us to demonstrate these achievements to our audience.

✽ Considering the context and the resources our characters have can help us create more believable stories.

Next step

In Chapter 13, we will return to the idea of everyone having a unique model of the world and explore how writers can gain a deeper insight into the way their characters see the world. We will also consider NLP's idea of taking multiple perspectives and how this can improve your understanding, add impact to your work and allow you to troubleshoot challenges.

13

Stepping into your characters' shoes

In this chapter you will learn about:

▶ *the concept of perceptual positions*

▶ *the differences between perceptual positions and points of view*

▶ *how taking different perceptual positions can be useful to the writer*

▶ *how multiple perceptual positions can be used to find the right point of view to tell a story, understand characters better, engage the audience more fully and add impact to your writing.*

Self-assessment: How do you spend time with your characters?

Do you ever:

1 Act through an important or difficult scene in your work as if you were one of the characters taking part in it?

2 Spend time 'getting into the head' of your characters before you start writing?

3 Write a scene from a non-viewpoint character's point of view to help you understand it, or write it better?

4 Step back and watch what is happening in a scene without feeling emotionally involved yourself or emotionally involved on behalf of any of your characters?

If you have answered 'no' to all of these questions, this chapter will show you how using **perceptual positions** can help to develop and improve your writing.

If you have answered 'yes' to any of the questions, then in some ways you are already working with perceptual positions. However, even if you have answered yes to all of the questions, this chapter can provide ways of troubleshooting challenges that may arise in your work.

Perceptual positions and the writer

Presupposition: Everyone lives in their own unique model of the world.

This presupposition reminds us that different people can and do interpret the same experiences and situations differently. NLP's concept of **perceptual positions** aims to help us understand other people's different perspectives and interpretations.

Writers naturally switch perspective when they move between thinking about different characters' thoughts, emotions and sensory perceptions or step back and watch their characters interact. However, deliberately thinking about the perceptual position we are taking can help us:

- enhance the detail in our work
- understand our characters more clearly
- understand our characters' experiences more clearly
- give greater impact to a scene
- find the voices of our characters
- find the right voice to tell a story
- find the right point of view to tell a story from.

NLP considers there are different 'perceptual positions'.

FIRST PERCEPTUAL POSITION

Taking first perceptual position means experiencing something from our own personal perspective alone. This includes what we perceive through our five senses, our thoughts, our emotions and the impact these perceptions have on our beliefs and values. First perceptual position means literally being inside our own body. Even seeing ourselves in our mind's eye means we are no longer in first perceptual position.

When we are writing, we can only truly take first perceptual position when we are writing about ourselves and our own experiences. However, taking first perceptual position can be useful to all writers in observing places and experiences in greater detail.

You have already used first perceptual position if you have worked through the exercise in 'Improve your understanding of what you are writing about' in Chapter 6 and/or the exercise in 'Improving your writing by strengthening your own representational systems' in Chapter 7. Both exercises lead you to take first perceptual position and observe in greater detail.

Try it now

Without first doing it, write a description of what you see, hear, feel and smell when you open your front door. When you have finished, go to your front door and open it. Consider what details you missed in your written description.

Remember this

Experiencing something from first perceptual position (i.e. experiencing what happens ourselves) can help us identify details we might otherwise miss.

▶ First perceptual position vs first person point of view

The idea of taking perceptual positions is related to, but should not be confused with the writing term **point of view**. When writers talk about 'point of view', they are talking about the viewpoint from which the audience is told a story.

First person point of view tells the story from the viewpoint of one of the story's characters. In prose this means the narrative is written in the first person. In films and television, it means using both first person point of view shots and shots where the viewpoint character is seen by the camera.

When a writer writes from first person point of view, they are imagining themselves inside the head of the point-of-view character, as is the audience when they read or watch the resulting story. Taking the first perceptual position means experiencing something from our own personal perspective alone. **First person point of view is therefore not the same as first perceptual position for either author or the audience.** The only exception to this is for the writer if they are writing about their own experience(s) in the first person and they are the viewpoint character. In this case, they are writing from first perceptual position.

Remember this

First perceptual position is not equivalent to first person point of view unless the work is autobiographical.

SECOND PERCEPTUAL POSITION

Second perceptual position is when we step into someone else's shoes and consider their view of the world. This can include empathizing with their emotions (emotional second position) and understanding their ideas, opinions and goals (intellectual second position). Therefore, when writers describe or consider what a character thinks, feels and takes in through their senses from that character's point of view, they are taking second perceptual position; imagining what it is like to be in someone else's shoes.

As we have already discussed, first person point of view tells the story from the viewpoint of one of the story's characters. If we compare point of view with second perceptual position, we can see that first person point of view is equivalent to second perceptual position for both writer and audience.

Remember this

When writers describe or consider what a character thinks, feels and takes in through their senses, they are taking the second perceptual position. Second perceptual position is therefore, in writing terms, first person point of view.

▶ Using second perceptual position

As well as writing from second perceptual position, i.e. first person point of view, writers can use second perceptual position to improve their work by deliberately taking this perspective and imagining themselves inside a character's body. By taking second perceptual position, we gain a better understanding of how that character perceives and processes a situation, learning new things about what they take in, think and feel.

Taking this idea a step further, many established writers don't just imagine what it's like to be a character; they imagine that they *are* the character and physically put themselves through the experiences they want to put their character through. The author Judy Waite uses a range of NLP techniques as part of both her teaching and her own professional practice. Talking about the techniques she's used, Judy says:

'I take myself places, in role, and see the world through my character's eyes. I once even auditioned to be in a boy band, as it was something my character had to do in the book – I didn't get the part (well, I am middle-aged and female) but it was an incredible way to experience the process.

*'More recently I spent a whole week in role, on a Greek island,
writing a summer romance. It's not just the big stuff – it's the
small things – butterflies. Birdsong. The way the sand feels
under your bare feet ...'*

Judy's experience shows us that taking second perceptual
position and physically working through a character's
experience doesn't just engage us with a character's thoughts
and emotions, but also the details they perceive. Understanding
details from our characters' perspective (second perceptual
position) is different from experiencing them from our own
perspective (first perceptual position), because our character's
mental filters are different from our own. For example, we may
personally smell salty sea air and remember happy holidays
with our grandparents. However, if our character got lost on
a beach as a young child, the smell of salty sea air may bring
back the terror of being lost and alone at a young age. Equally,
when she is in love, Judy Waite's island romance character
will feel differently about her surroundings and may focus on
different details than if Judy was writing about a character who
had just been bereaved.

 Try it now

Imagine you are a young girl in love. Take a moment or two to think about
who this young girl is, and then write a brief description of the view from
the nearest window from her point of view.

Now imagine you are a 40-year-old woman who was happily married
but has been suddenly widowed. Take a moment or two to think about
who this woman is and the circumstances of her loss, and then write
a brief description of the view from the same window from her point
of view.

Of course it's not always practical, possible or advisable to
put yourself through some experiences, especially if they could
impact on your personal wellbeing or safety. However, we can
work to recreate as much of an experience as we can within the
bounds of possibility and personal safety.

Try it now

Consider the first scene of your work in progress. Provided it doesn't put you at any risk, place yourself in the physical position that the viewpoint character is in at the start. Imagine what their senses are taking in. Match their breathing rate. Pull their thoughts into your mind and their feelings and emotions into your mind and body. Now move through the scene with them, physically and mentally: think, feel, move and speak as they do.

Rewrite the scene using what you have experienced and anything useful you have learned.

This exercise will prove even more useful if you carry it out in the actual place or scenario where the character has their experience. However, always ensure that you don't put yourself in any potentially dangerous or illegal situations or scenarios, or cause anything negative to happen to any person, animal or property.

Key idea

Experiencing something that happens to one of our characters from second perceptual position (i.e. imagining yourself as that character and experiencing what happens) can help us gain more insight into and deeper understanding of how that character perceives that experience.

THIRD PERCEPTUAL POSITION

Taking third perceptual position is when we mentally step outside an interaction between ourselves and someone else and watch what is happening from a detached perspective. It is only writers who are writing autobiographically that can do this, because they themselves are in the picture. However, a writer would still not write their story from third perceptual position, as a detached perspective would result in an unengaging piece of writing.

Writers never take a completely dispassionate view when they are writing. This is because we usually tell a story through the eyes of one or more of the story's characters. Even if we use an unseen narrator, they still tell our audience about their perspective, inevitably conveying how they think, feel and perceive the world.

Because the camera is an object that has no attachment to what is happening, it may seem that in film and television, when there is no narrator, a detached point of view is taken. However, films, TV dramas and even documentaries are crafted to encourage the audience to see certain perspectives and points of view. In other words, it is not the camera that chooses what to show us, but those writing and making the film.

Case study

If we return to the scene in the Chapter 7 case study and write it from a detached perspective (rather than using an unseen narrator), the story becomes a list of bland observations, meaning is lost and what is happening becomes more a matter of guesswork or the reader's opinion.

Original paragraph

Amy warmed her hands against the china mug and stared across the empty coffee shop. If only Archie had still been here.

A waitress dropped a mug on the tiled floor behind her. But Amy was so lost in thought, she didn't even hear it smash or notice the shards of china skidding past her shoes. She blew the froth from the top of her coffee and sipped the dark liquid. If only Archie had still been here.

Detached perspective

Amy held her hands against the mug and stared across the empty coffee shop.

A waitress dropped a mug on the tiled floor behind her. Amy didn't appear to hear it break or notice the broken pieces as they moved past her shoes. She blew the froth from the top of her mug. There was a black liquid underneath. Amy put her lips to the edge of the mug and drank the liquid.

▶ Using third perceptual position

Although writers never write from a detached position, it can be useful to think dispassionately about a scene we are writing by modifying the idea of third perceptual position and taking a detached view of our characters' interactions. This can help us 'get out of the head(s)' of our point-of-view character(s) and learn more about all of our characters, our plot and our settings.

Try it now

Consider a scene from your work in progress in which three or more characters interact with one another. Close your eyes and play the scene through in your imagination without entering the head of any of your characters.

Do you learn anything new about your characters or identify something you can improve or add about:

❋ the setting?
❋ the way the characters interact with one another?
❋ what your non-point-of-view characters are doing when the point-of-view character isn't paying attention to them?
❋ your point-of-view character?
❋ your point-of-view character's body language?

▶ Third perceptual position vs third person point of view

In prose, third person point of view is told by an invisible narrator who tells the story in the third person. The range of third person point of view runs from 'close third person' – where the author shares the perceptions, thoughts and feelings of only one character – to 'omniscient' – where the narrator can describe anywhere and anyone's thoughts, feelings and perceptions.

Third person point of view is therefore never the same as third perceptual position, because it directly reveals the thoughts, perceptions and feelings of one or more characters, while third perceptual position takes a detached perspective. Even if a story is autobiographical and the writer is stepping back and writing about themselves from third person point of view, they would never take third perceptual position because it comes from a detached point of view. This would result in a story that was about as interesting as a washing machine manual.

Remember this

Third perceptual position is not equivalent to third person point of view.

Note: There is a huge amount to be learned about point of view and this chapter only intends to clarify the difference between the NLP concept of perceptual position and the writing term 'point of view'.

Key idea

The terms *perceptual position* and *point of view* mean different things and are **not** interchangeable.

Your characters' perceptual positions

People can be much better at taking one perceptual position than another. For example, some people are very good at seeing their own point of view but find it hard to imagine themselves in other people's shoes. However, just like real people, some characters will be much better at seeing their own perspective, some much better at seeing others' perspectives and some good at seeing both their own and others' perspectives. Furthermore, unless something happens to change a character's ability to take different perceptual positions, they will continue to predominantly use the same position(s)

Using multiple perceptual positions

NLP explores people's challenges by getting them to take multiple perceptual positions. The creators of NLP have developed two main methods of switching between perceptual positions: one for dealing with relationships, and one for preparing for potentially difficult business meetings. These are not of particular use to writers, but the idea of moving between perceptual positions can be useful in:

▶ helping to find the right point of view to tell a story from

▶ identifying how to give greater impact to a scene

- engaging your audience more fully in your story

- understanding your characters more clearly.

Finding the right point of view to tell your story from

Sometimes a story can only be told from one character's point of view or it is obvious which character(s) should narrate a story. However, if you are unsure whose point of view to use, if a story doesn't seem to be working, or you're struggling to get the voice of a story, it's worth checking out the possible points of view you could be telling your story from. It's also worth experimenting with different characters' perspectives at the outset of developing a story to:

- get to know your characters and their relationships

- consider whether it would be best to use first or third person point of view.

EXPERIMENTING WITH PERSPECTIVE AND POINT OF VIEW

1 Write the opening scene of your story – or just the beginning of it if it's very long – in first person prose from the point of view of each of your main characters. If none of the people you believe to be your main characters is in the opening scene, use instead the first scene in which they appear (but also consider why none of your main characters is in the opening scene – see Chapter 11).

2 Ask yourself the following questions.

- Whose voice is most engaging?

- Who is most invested emotionally, intellectually and/or financially in what is happening in this scene?

- Who has most to gain from the events that happen in my story?

- Who has most to lose from the events that happen in my story?

- Who is most invested emotionally, intellectually and/or financially in the changes/events that happen throughout the story?

- Who grows most/learns most through this story?

▶ For each character, ask:

▷ how much of the 'real action' of the story do they experience?

▷ how well-positioned is **this** character to narrate the whole story?

3 Use your answers to these questions to help you identify whose eyes it would be best to show the story through. Remember, there are no right or wrong answers and you may decide to show the story through the eyes of one or more characters.

4 Once you have decided whose eyes it would best to show the story through, if you have not already done so, write the first scene in the third person from their point of view.

5 Compare the first person and third person scenes you wrote from the perspective of the person you have considered. Which is better? Is this likely to be the case throughout the book?

6 Write the final scene in both the first person and the third person from the same character's point of view. Do you still think this is the best point of view to use?

▶ If your answer is 'yes', consider whether you need to use or feel your work would be better if you used more than one point of view.

▶ If your answer is 'no', repeat steps 3 to 6.

Note: The more point-of-view characters you have in your story, the harder it will be for your audience to connect with them and the easier it will be for the audience to become confused. However, multiple points of view can be very successful.

Giving a scene greater impact

Sometimes our work feels flat and/or our characters feel as if they're going through the motions rather than living their experience. If you find this happening, try these explorations.

▶ **Exploration 1**

1 Identify a scene that you feel needs more life or where one or more characters feel as if they're not fully engaged with what is happening.

2   Identify which characters aren't working properly or feel insufficiently effective?

3   Put your own thoughts and feeling to one side. Take up the posture and physical stance of the point-of-view character at the beginning of the scene.

4   Take second perceptual position by imaging you are that character – imagining you are feeling the emotions they feel, experiencing any sensory input they are receiving and having the thoughts that they are having.

5   Run through the scene in your mind's eye as if you were that person. If it doesn't put you at any sort of risk, move physically with them too.

6   Note what reactions you feel and thoughts you have.

7   Run though the scene once more to check you haven't missed anything.

8   Literally give yourself a shake, move your thoughts back to yourself.

9   Chose another character from the scene and move physically to another place in the room.

10 Once more, put your own thoughts and feelings to one side. Take up the posture and physical stance of your chosen character at the beginning of the scene.

11 Repeat steps 3–7 for this character.

12 Shake yourself again, return to your own thoughts, and then repeat steps 3–9 for every other character who engages with any of the other characters in the scene.

When you have considered all the active characters within the scene, ask yourself the following questions.

▶ Are all these characters sufficiently developed? If not, develop them further.

▶ Do any of the characters need to have a bigger part in the scene? If so, get them more involved? (See below.)

▶ Is the audience being shown enough of every characters' thoughts, emotions, actions and reactions in what I have already written? If not, show more – but don't go over the top – and take care not to switch point of view into the heads of any of the non-point-of-view characters.

▶ Are any of my characters too similar? If they are, consider how you could make them more distinct from each other. Also consider whether you need both of these characters in the scene or even in your story. Could they be blended to create one character?

▶ Could I cut any of these characters from the scene without them being missed?

Reflect on this exploration and consider what changes you want to make.

▶ Exploration 2

This is useful for getting characters more involved in a scene or adding greater interest/connection for your audience.

Take second perceptual position for the point-of-view character, i.e. inside the head of your point-of-view character, and consider what happens if you:

▶ add/amplify their emotions, e.g. give them reason to be (more) frightened, (more) excited, (more) passionate, etc.

▶ add more description of thoughts, emotions, actions, reactions or atmosphere.

If you haven't done so already, what happens if you:

▶ confront any of their values that link to what is happening in the scene?

▶ confound any of their beliefs that link to what is happening in the scene?

▶ add humour to the scene?

Reflect on this exploration and consider what changes you want to make.

► **Exploration 3**

If a story or scene lacks impact, consider:

► whether the point-of-view character is sufficiently involved and invested in what is happening. If they are not, consider how you can make them more involved/invested.

► whether the point-of-view character is the right person to be telling your story. See the earlier section 'Finding the right point of view to tell your story from.

► whether moving one or more of your characters to a different location or showing the scene from a different angle in the same location will increase its impact.

► whether placing your audience closer to or further away from the action will increase the impact.

Reflect on this exploration and consider what changes you want to make.

Remember this

Whenever you make changes, always ensure anything you add or change is in keeping with your plot and writing style. Also, always ensure your characters behave congruently with who they are.

Understanding your characters better

Sometimes we feel as if our characters are running away with our story and 'doing their own thing', or at least trying to. At other times, a character can feel as if they're only going through the motions. If you face either of these challenges and you're happy that you have shown enough of what your characters are experiencing:

1 Pick a scene in which you are having this challenge – preferably a scene where the character you are having problems with is interacting with only one other character.

2 Leaving your own thoughts and feelings to one side, take the third perceptual position and run the scene through in your mind as if it were a movie – but ensure that you remain detached.

3 Note what happens, what each character says and how each character reacts. (You may wish to run through the scene more than once, making notes during or after each run.)

4 Literally give yourself a shake and move your thoughts back to yourself.

5 Identify from your notes exactly what you saw that you aren't happy about within the scene; what does each character say and how does each character react?

6 Now move to another part of the room. Take up the posture and physical stance the character you are unhappy with takes at the beginning of the scene. Image you are that character and settle into the emotions they feel, the thoughts they are having, and imagine any sensory input they are receiving.

7 Run through the scene in your mind's eye as if you were that person. If it doesn't put you at any sort of risk, move physically with them too.

8 Note what reactions you feel and what thoughts you have at the point(s) in the scene you aren't happy with. Run though the scene more than once if necessary.

9 Literally give yourself a shake, move your thoughts back to yourself and move physically back to the place in the room where you were initially.

10 Reflect on what is happening – or not happening – inside your character at the point(s) you are unhappy with. For example, you might recognize that your character holds a belief that is causing them to behave in a certain way or that one of their values is being confronted and they are not reacting appropriately. What you want to do about your findings will depend on what you uncover and it could lead to you redeveloping or even replacing a character.

11 If you can't identify why a character is behaving the way they are, consider whether your character is sufficiently developed or whether you need to do more work on developing them.

Focus points

The main points to remember from this chapter are:

* Experiencing something from first perceptual position (i.e. experiencing what happens ourselves) can help us to identify details we might otherwise miss.

* When writers consider what a character thinks, feels and takes in through their senses, they are taking second perceptual position and imagining what it is like to be in someone else's shoes.

* Experiencing something that happens to one of our characters from the second perceptual position (i.e. imagining yourself as that character and experiencing what happens) can help us gain insight into and a deeper understanding of how that character perceives that experience.

* The terms 'perceptual position' and 'point of view' mean different things and are not interchangeable.

* Considering scenes from different perspectives can be very useful when writers are developing their work.

Guide to terminology

anchor – a stimulus that triggers a particular action or state without us even thinking about it.

belief – something we believe to be true, whether it is true or not.

Big Chunk thinking – thinking that considers the bigger picture.

chunking down – increasing the level of detail.

chunking up – decreasing the level of detail.

core value – a value that is important to every area of our life.

deletion – ignoring or deleting all or part of an experience.

distortion – changing our understanding or interpretation of an experience from what actually happened.

frame – a way of looking at something; a particular point of view.

generalization – extrapolating one or more specific experience(s) to represent a whole group or class.

matching and mirroring – matching and reflecting another person's behaviour, language, beliefs or values when in communication with them.

metaphor – an image, story or tangible entity used to describe or represent something in a way that is abstract or not literally applicable.

meta programs – a way of describing approaches we take to thinking about situations and challenges. Meta programs generally come in pairs of bipolar opposites.

modality – one of our five senses.

modelling – observing or experiencing the way someone else does something and doing it that way yourself.

NLP – Neuro-linguistic Programming:

➤ **Neuro** refers to our neurology and the way our brains process information received from our five senses.

- **Linguistic** relates to our use of language systems to understand and store information about the world and to communicate with others and with ourselves. This includes not just the spoken and written word, but also symbolism and non-verbal signals.

- **Programming** means the way we store, use and act on the information our brains take in. The NLP concept of programming is taken from information processing and computer science, seeing analogies between the way we use our brains and how computer software can be upgraded or new software can be installed.

non-verbal – any way people communicate other than through the words they use. This includes posture, movements, gestures, vocal variations, breathing, changes in skin tone, facial expressions, proximity and appearence.

outcome – what we get as a result of our actions.

perceptual positions:

- **first perceptual position** – seeing things from our own personal perspective.

- **second perceptual position** – mentally stepping into someone else's shoes and considering their thoughts, feelings and view of the world.

- **third perceptual position** – mentally stepping outside an interaction between ourselves and someone else and observing what is happening from a detached perspective.

presupposition – something we take as a 'given' and accept to be true, even though it may not be.

proximity – the distance between people in a social situation.

rapport – how well we understand and communicate with others. When we have strong rapport, we feel as if we are 'on the same wavelength' as someone else and communication flows easily. When there is a lack of rapport, we struggle to communicate or understand someone.

representational system – a system within our brain that uses one of our senses to recreate real or imagined events.

Small Chunk thinking – thinking that focuses on details.

state – the sum total of our reaction to everything we perceive and the way we are processing it at any given moment. For the purposes of writing, this means how we are currently feeling.

strategy – the thought processes that leads us through the way we do something.

submodalities – distinctions of form or structure – rather than content – within a sensory representational system.

VAKOG – an acronym used to refer collectively to the five representational systems. It stands for: Visual (seeing); Auditory (hearing); Kinaesthetic (feeling and touching); Olfactory (smell); Gustatory (tasting).

value – a fundamental principle that we believe it important to uphold. Values are deeply rooted beliefs that are far less easily changed than a lot of the other beliefs we hold. Values are identified by simple descriptors such as respect, honesty, ambition, adventure, support, peace, creativity, individuality, loyalty.

verbal – the words we use when we speak.

well-formed outcome – NLP's method of focusing on what people want or need to achieve. Well-formed outcomes are a very precise and structured approach to planning achievement that fit nine conditions which are designed to increase the likelihood of the success.

Further resources

From the author

Hill, B. (2011). *Coach Yourself to Writing Success*. London: Teach Yourself, Hodder.

For information on workshops and courses run by the author, visit www.thewritecoach.co.uk

Follow Bekki on Twitter @bekkiwritecoach

Basic NLP

Bavister, S. & Vickers, A. (2010). Essential NLP. Hodder: Teach Yourself.

Burton, K. & Ready, R. (2008). Neuro-linguistic Programming for Dummies. John Wiley & Sons.

Meta programs

Rose-Charvet, S. (1997). Words That Change Minds. Kendall Hunt.

Proxemics

Hall, E. T. (1998). The Hidden Dimension. Bantam Doubleday Dell Publishing Group.

Writing fiction

Bell, J. & Magrs, P. (Eds), (2001). The Creative Writing Coursebook. Macmillan.

Corner, H. & Weatherly, L. (2010). How to Write a Blockbuster. Hodder: Teach Yourself.

Card, O. S. (1999). Characters and Viewpoint. Writer's Digest Books.

McKee, R. (1999). Story: Substance, Structure, Style and the Principles of Screenwriting. Methuen.

Tobias, R. (2003). 20 Master Plots (and How to Build Them). Writer's Digest Books.

Writing magazines

Mslexia
www.mslexia.co.uk

Writers' Forum
www.writers-forum.com

Writers' News and Writing Magazine
www.writersnews.co.uk

Writing groups and associations

The Crime Writers' Association
www.thecwa.co.uk

The Romantic Novelists Association
www.rna-uk.org

The Society of Children's Book Writers and Illustrators (SCBWI)
www.scbwi.org
www.scbwi.jimdo.com

The Society of Authors
www.thesocietyofauthors.net

National Association of Writers' Groups
www.nawg.co.uk

Find a writers' group in your area

Useful websites
www.writerscircles.com
www.writewords.org.uk

Index